The
Molding *of a*
Champion

Helping Your Child Shape a Winning Destiny

Dr. Gregory Jantz
with Ann McMurray

First printing: August 2006
Second printing: August 2007

ISBN-13: 978-0-89221-648-2
ISBN-10: 0-89221-648-4
Library of Congress Number: 2006928672

Cover by Janell Robertson

Unless otherwise noted, all Scripture is from the New International Version of the Bible.

Printed in the United States of America

For information regarding author interviews, please contact the publicity department at (870) 438-5288.

Please visit our website for other great titles:
www.newleafpress.net

New Leaf Press
A Division of New Leaf Publishing Group

Dedication

To my Christ-champions,
Gregg and Benjamin

Acknowledgment

Parenting and molding champions entrusted to us is certainly the work of a dedicated spiritual team. It's the same with writing this book. I am blessed daily by a God-assembled team of leaders. My deepest appreciation is extended to Ann McMurray, Laura Minor, Mike Weiford, and Shelley Miller. Foremost, I wish to acknowledge my wife, LaFon, who faithfully lives out her destiny as a champion of God — in our marriage, our family, and in our vision for the Center as "a place of hope."

Contents

Foreword

As a husband, father, and pastor of several thousand people, I rejoice with Dr. Jantz in the writing of this book. First of all, because the subject is so needed and so important in our society today, but also because I know Gregg, his wife, and two boys. This is not a book of theories and clinical analysis. You will find real life truths in this work; day-to-day life with Dad, Mom, and growing children. Set in a biblical perspective, the message is strong and clear.

There are insights that will make you a better person and parent; wisdom that will help you understand what you and your children are going through; practical, real-world knowledge that gives you simple steps to follow; and biblical insights that will encourage and spiritually empower you to raise your family for God.

Raising children is our highest calling on this planet. Based on the amount of pain and struggle we have in our families today, it may be our most difficult calling. Almost anyone can have a baby, but it is not easy to mold a champion. Dr. Jantz shows us what every child can be and then gives the practical steps we can take to help him or her get there. So often we hear parenting advice from the talk show host who has no children, isn't married, or has full-time nannies that handle everything. This work is from the heart of a dad who is in the trenches of parenting every day and knows the daily process of parenting. This is not popular psychology and quaint ramblings that are packaged to sell a program. You will read truth, real-life testimonies, and biblical applications that will make a difference in your life and family.

I love the Bible stories of Deborah and Samson. You will see how their challenges and successes translate into wonderful life lessons for we who are in the process of molding our champions. There are no better lives to learn from than those God chose to be part of His Holy Word. Dr. Jantz's practical and spiritual insights will inspire you and give you ideas to help your children be all they can be. You will also read of present-day champions who have risen out of divorce, despair, poverty, and other barriers of our world to be great people. Some of these are in our church and we see their lives in action. Others you have heard of, and you will be encouraged by the stories of their growth and success.

Whatever age and stage of life you and your family are in, I know *The Molding of a Champion* will lift you to your next season. That's what Dr. Jantz is all about, and that is what this book is all about: lifting you and giving you tools to go to your highest place in life. God is not holding you back. Don't let the world and the problems you face hold you back. Be the person and the parent God has called you to be and help your children be the champions God has called them to be. I know you will be blessed, and I pray your family will be changed as you enjoy the pages of *The Molding of a Champion*.

Casey Treat
Senior Pastor, Christian Faith Center
Seattle, WA

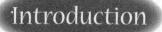

Our Children as Conquerers

I'm a parent. I have two young sons, both identical in worth, each different in design. Gregg, my oldest, is a very eager, serious child of six. He loves structure and order. You can see the wheels turning in his mind, with a great desire to understand. In essence, Gregg is very much a first child. He interacts smoothly with the adult world around him and has a great desire to *know*. Benjamin, on the other hand, at three, has a great desire to *do*. He is energy-incarnate. It's hard to see the wheels turning in his mind because he hardly ever stands still long enough. Gregg adapts to the world. The world tends to adapt to Benjamin. He is like a force of nature, a gyroscope of life that bends the world inward with gravitational pull — and, like a whirlwind, he tends to leave destruction in his wake!

Both my children are amazing. When I look at them, I feel so many overwhelming emotions — from love and pride to fear and apprehension. I'll bet you feel the same way about yours. The love you feel is deep-rooted, almost organic. Yet, at the same time, you experience apprehension over their well-being. You wonder, *what does the future hold for my child?*

You would think being a Christian makes parenting easier. After all, we understand God's protection and providence better than secular parents, who tackle the job of raising a child without spiritual foundations. As Christians, we see the spiritual foundations but we also see the spiritual warfare taking place over the souls of our children, something secular parents may perceive dimly at best.

You would think, for me, being a counselor with a degree in psychology would make it easier. After all, I've been trained to understand human nature and action. As a counselor, however, I've experienced the worst of that nature and action. I've seen how the errors and actions of parents — even well-intentioned ones — can damage their children long into adulthood.

What it all boils down to, I think, is no matter our backgrounds, we're all parents, trying the best we know to raise our kids. I want my children to be healthy mentally, spiritually, and physically. I want them to succeed in society and grow up to be mature and happy. No different from you.

I want something else; I want my children to understand they have been designed and designated as God's champions in this world; this is Gregg and Benjamin's special destiny. This knowledge is a large source of my joy; it's also a large source of apprehension — *what if I mess up what God intended?* There — I've publicly laid out a major private fear. It's a fear that's private to me but also pretty universal among Christian parents. If that's what prompted you to pick up and read this book, believe me, I understand; it's what prompted me to write it. As parents and Christians, then, we're all on the same page. From that page through the rest of these pages, we're going to explore God's Word, our hearts, our experiences, and biblical examples to help better understand how we can help mold our children into spiritual champions who are conquerors for Christ.

Our Children As Champions

Following, I'd like to outline for you what this book is about. It's about children and it's for parents. It will speak to parents of children of different ages, of both genders, of different personalities. I specifically address parents, but the concepts presented are applicable to extended family, grandparents, and loving caregivers of children. I trust you to be able to modify and adapt this information in such a way as to maximize its use for you and your situation. I trust God to speak to you through these words and reveal His truth — truth about your child and truth about yourself. After all, it is in loving and caring for a child that we come to understand fundamental truths about God our Father. It's like we try out our own small version of a God-suit when we cradle our children for the first time. We get to feel as human parents — in the tiniest of ways — what God feels like as our Heavenly Father. Through children, we come to appreciate God. Through children, we come to understand God. Loving and learning. Caring and comprehension. In this way, God heaps blessings upon us when we become parents.

I've tried to section the book so you can read it over once, and then refer to specific sections or chapters later on, as you have need. Because children don't grow up overnight, this book will be handy to keep around. You may be reading it as your kids are toddlers and realize it would be good to read it again when they're in elementary school. Each chapter begins with a passage of Scripture and ends with a prayer. That's kind of what my life is like with my kids — I start each day with the promises of God about my children and end each day with an earnest appeal to God on behalf of my kids.

Section 1: Laying the Foundations

Each parent has been given the gift of a child. Your child today is God's champion tomorrow. Champions must be cultivated and nurtured. As a parent, it is your privilege to mentor this champion, who will go out and conquer for Christ. Saving the world is a big job, so it's good to be prepared.

The theme verses for Section 1 are Romans 8:28–39:

> And we know that in all things God works for the good of those who love him, who have been called according to his purpose. For those God foreknew he also predestined to be conformed to the likeness of his Son, that he might be the firstborn among many brothers. And those he predestined, he also called; those he called, he also justified; those he justified, he also glorified. What, then, shall we say in response to this? If God is for us, who can be against us? He who did not spare his own Son, but gave him up for us all — how will he not also, along with him, graciously give us all things? Who will bring any charge against those whom God has chosen? It is God who justifies. Who is he that condemns? Christ Jesus, who died — more than that, who was raised to life — is at the right hand of God and is also interceding for us. Who shall separate us from the love of Christ? Shall trouble or hardship or persecution or famine or nakedness or danger or sword? As it is written: "For your sake we face death all day long; we are considered as sheep to be slaughtered." No, in all these things we are more than conquerors through him who loved us.

Chapter 1: *Preparing Yourself* — As I think about my children as champions for God, I recognize that, as a parent, their training and nurture starts with me. God has entrusted these precious souls into my care. This is an overwhelming task and, in order to prepare them, I need to first prepare myself. Using the example of Hannah and Samuel, this chapter will encourage all of us to anticipate and appreciate the consequences of truly turning our children over to God.

Chapter 2: *Preparing Your Family* — Children exist within the framework of immediate and extended family. Gregg and Benjamin relate to me, their mother, LaFon, their grandparents, aunts, and uncles. It is through this family framework that children receive much of their vision of who they are in the world. In order to mold a champion, the family must view the child as a champion. Using both Old and New Testament examples, we'll look at how molding champions is really a family affair.

Chapter 3: *Preparing Your Child* — In order for children to see themselves as champions for the Lord, they must understand the nature of the battle, whom they are fighting, what they are fighting for, and the resources at their disposal. This chapter will use Ephesians 6:10–18, outlining the armor of God. This chapter will also help you create a personalized Championship Creed for your child.

Section 2: Finding Their Fruit

The gifts of our children are not always immediately visible or known. Sometimes they require a journey of discovery to identify their gifts. It can be difficult to remember that it's not a question of whether they have gifts but what those gifts are.

The theme verse for Section 2 is 2 Corinthians 9:8:

> And God is able to make all grace abound to you, so that in all things at all times, having all that you need, you will abound in every good work.

Chapter 4: *Cultivating Universal Gifts* — Each person is blessed by God with universal gifts through the Holy Spirit. This chapter will look at how the fruit of the Spirit from Galatians 5:22–23 can be awakened in our children. (It will also serve as a reminder of how important these attributes are in parents as well!)

Chapter 5: *Identifying Personal Gifts* — There are universal gifts and then there are personal gifts, bestowed by God to individuals in order to advance His will. Using Psalm 139 and Ephesians 4, this chapter will provide you with practical ways to identify personal gifts in your children.

Section 3: Molding the Whole Champion

Your child exists as an emotional, physical, intellectual, and spiritual being. All of these aspects will contribute to the expression of their God-given gifts. Like seeds, these gifts are planted within the very core of your child. In order for them to fully flower, the whole person must be cultivated.

The theme verse for Section 3 is Mark 12:30:

> Love the Lord your God with all your heart and with all your soul and with all your mind and with all your strength.

Chapter 6: *Whole Hearted* — Our children are powered by their emotional makeup. It's vital, then, that they *recognize* and *regulate* their own emotions, and *read* and *respond* to the emotions of others. In addition, children of faith have been set apart, by God and by the culture. Both of these situations have emotional impacts on children. In order to accept and adjust to their faith, children need to develop a healthy emotional foundation. It's vital that our children develop emotional insight, to better understand themselves and the world they live in. In this chapter, we'll look at the life of the champion destined to pave the way for Jesus — John the Baptist.

Chapter 7: *Spiritual Depth* — The bedrock foundation of the life of a child should be spiritual development and a growing relationship and belief in God and Christ. By looking at the parable of the seed and the sower in Luke 8, we'll discover how important childhood is for developing the right kind of spiritual soil. We'll see that spiritual development establishes the context through which a child becomes God's champion in this world. Jesus began His training to be God's champion even as a young child. In a similar way, we can help our children develop a deep, dependent faith and trust in God, and a firm belief in the future He has for them.

Chapter 8: *Intelligent Faith* — It is one thing to receive a gift; it is another to have the tools to implement and apply the gift. Children need to develop their minds — their intellect — in order to be ready to give a ready response or use their gift when the time is right. We are told to love the Lord with all of our heart, soul, mind, and strength. If the heart is emotion, soul is spirit, strength is body, then mind is intellect. Using various scriptural examples from the life and writings of the apostle Paul, this chapter will look at how important it is to prepare your child to develop an *intelligent* faith.

Chapter 9: *Strong in the Lord* — God has given children purpose in His kingdom, accomplished through their physical bodies. As a temple of the Holy Spirit, a child's body is an important conduit through which the child's faith is lived out. This chapter will stress the importance of safeguarding the physical well-being of our children and highlight the example of Old Testament heroes Daniel, Shadrach, Meshach, and Abednego.

Section 4: Support

My sons, Gregg and Benjamin, are very different from each other. What works with one doesn't automatically work with the other. I have to approach them as individuals, not only in teaching or discipline, but also in how I show and provide support. Support is only effective if it is tailored to the child. After all, it doesn't help to put a goldfish in an ocean or a tuna in a river. Both are fish, but they need different types of environments to support them.

The theme verse for Section 4 is 2 Chronicles 6:30–31:

> Listen from your home in heaven, forgive and reward us: reward each life and circumstance, for you know each life from the inside (you're the only one with such inside knowledge!), so they'll live before you in lifelong reverence and believing obedience on this land you gave our ancestors (TM).

Chapter 10: *Support for Girls* — Now, granted, I have sons, but I'm married to someone's daughter. My wife, LaFon, is an amazing champion for God, no less so because she's female. God assigned different roles for both genders but all children can be mighty warriors for God. It can be difficult for parents, sometimes, to view their daughters as warriors, as champions, as conquerors. The fault lies in how we view the battle. In this chapter, we'll use the story of

Deborah and other women of faith to help us understand the courage and conviction God gives to our daughters.

Chapter 11: *Support for Boys* — It might seem that society already prepares boys to be warriors. Our culture today, however, too often sees boys from an adversarial viewpoint, ascribing God-given boy traits to abnormal pathology. For boys to grow and mature, support must be provided that is gender-sensitive. In our culture today, especially in our education system, boys are tolerated, at best, and medicated, at worst. We seem to have come full circle in the eyes of some; instead of girls being considered inferior to boys, boys are now considered defective, inferior to girls. Making boys feel defective sabotages their ability to see themselves as champions. This chapter will highlight the latest neurological research into the boy brain. It will use the relationship between Elijah and Elisha to illustrate the time-honored tradition of male bonding and mentoring.

Chapter 12: *Support Across the Ages* — The joy of being a champion for God isn't deferred until adulthood. God can and does use children to further His will, to defend His causes, and showcase His glory. Children of any age can be confident God-champions, as they grow at school, in the community, and at home. This chapter will look at biblical examples of children, younger adolescents, and teens to remind us how God can use the open heart of a child, whatever the age. In addition, there will be plenty of practical strategies for how to show your support as your child moves from age to age.

Chapter 13: *Support for the Challenging Child* — Some kids are simply more challenging than others. Some kids have more challenging periods in their lives. It's important to maintain our support and encouragement — our steadfast belief in them — even during challenging times or with especially challenging children. Using the story of the Prodigal Son, this chapter will help us look at the importance of a parent's, especially a father's, steadfast belief in their children.

Chapter 14: *Where to Go From Here* — Just as raising a champion takes more than one day or month or year, it's also going to take more than one book. Or, it's going to take several books all based on one book, the Bible. This is one, but there are many others written by spiritual, godly men and women. In this last chapter, I've reviewed over 40 books that you can choose from as the next step in your sacred duty of molding a champion for God. There are books for your personal growth, specific to a gender or age and, oddly enough, quite a few selections on how to deal with challenging children! I've written just a short paragraph on each, giving you a synopsis and the information you'll need to find the book to further your study. Most of all, it's meant as an encouragement to keep going. For parents, I think two books are essential for any desktop or nightstand — the Bible and a personal study to strengthen your parenting. This chapter is my way of saying, "Way to go! Now, keep going!"

Laying the Foundations

I f you're going to build a house or a deck, a skyscraper or a life of a champion, you need to first lay the foundation. Nothing illustrates this concept more than that catchy little Sunday school song about the wise and the foolish man. It's based upon Jesus' parable, found in Matthew 7:24–27. Kids love to sing that song (adults, too, I admit!) just to get to the part where they get to yell "Splat!" when the foolish man's house on the sand gets destroyed. It's a funny little song about a fundamental principle. To build a deep, solid foundation of faith in your child, you must engage in some "site prep." You need to make sure it's built on the Rock and not on the sand of this world. Sometimes, that means you have to move — either your beliefs, or values, or even your family.

With a foundation, it's all about the site prep. This first section is going to help you make sure you've laid the proper groundwork for this monumental task of molding a champion. Layer by layer, you'll make sure you've done what you need to, from the ground up. Of course, prep work is often tedious, detailed work that can lack the pizzazz of the final touches. That's kind of parenting in a nutshell. As much as day-to-day parenting and prep can appear a drudgery at times, don't skip this step; your child is a very important project to the master building. Remember, you may be the site manager, but you're not the owner of the building. You're in charge of the project, but you answer to a higher authority where your children are concerned.

Each child is a gift from God to you, as a parent. Your child today is God's champion tomorrow. Champions must be cultivated and nurtured. As a parent, it is your privilege to mentor this champion, who will go out and conquer for Christ. Saving the world is a big job, so it's good to be prepared.

In order to help you recognize the nature of the task — the building, the molding ahead — listen to the prep work God has already done where your child is concerned, in Romans 8:28–39:

> And we know that in all things God works for the good of those who love him, who have been called according to his purpose. For those God foreknew he also predestined to be conformed to the likeness of his Son, that he might be the firstborn among many brothers. And those he predestined, he also called; those he called, he also justified; those he justified, he also glorified. What, then, shall we say in response to this? If God is for us, who can be against us? He who did not spare his own Son, but gave him up for us all — how will he not also, along with him, graciously give us all things? Who will bring any charge against those whom God has chosen? It is God who justifies. Who is he that condemns? Christ Jesus, who died — more than that, who was raised to life — is at the right hand of God and is also interceding for us. Who shall separate us from the love of Christ? Shall trouble or hardship or persecution or famine or nakedness or danger or sword? As it is written: "For your sake we face death all day long; we are considered as sheep to be slaughtered." No, in all these things we are more than conquerors through him who loved us.

Chapter 1

Preparing Yourself

If anyone causes one of these little ones who believe in me to sin, it would be better for him to be thrown into the sea with a large millstone tied around his neck (Mark 9:42).

I chose this verse as a reminder of the eternal significance of our job as parents — both to them and to us. This isn't a casual pursuit or something that can be undertaken as a hobby. It's an all-or-nothing, whatever-it-takes kind of commitment. It isn't something you can fit in around everything else in your life. It isn't an occasional occupation. Whether or not you live with your children 24/7, you must be a parent 24/7. As long as that child is young, all the way through adulthood, you're on the hook. Personally, I wouldn't have my life any other way.

The Whole World in a Tiny Hand

Have you ever seen one of those pictures of a tiny fist grasping just the finger of an adult? It's a beautiful depiction of the love of a parent and the trust of an infant. A tiny hand curled reflexively around the larger finger. The strength of a parent, the fragility of a child. It is amazing to realize, then, that God, who designed that tiny little hand, chooses to place the entire world into it. He's done it since the beginning of time. He did it through His Son; he does it through our own children. Looking at our world, though, it just doesn't seem possible that God would entrust so much to seemingly so little — the whole world in a tiny hand. Our paradox is answered in 1 Corinthians 1:27, which says "But God chose the foolish things of the world to shame the wise; God chose the weak things of the world to shame the strong."

That tiny fist isn't just a fist; it's the fist of a champion. This is God's intent and design. It is also his intent and design to put that tiny champion into your care. It's our job as parents to help nurture this champion. We may not know specifically yet the task God has laid out for our children but, as believers, we already know where the battle lines are drawn. For this is a battle, and champions are needed to overcome the world.

This section starts out with a rather lengthy Scripture reading from Romans 8. Now, you may have gotten a little distracted because it's a long reading and it takes a while to get to the "more than conquerors" part. But, when you did, didn't it make your heart soar! We love the thought of ourselves — and our children — in this context, as conquerors, as victorious — and we are! That's the finale we're all hoping for, the big finish where our children are victorious in the Lord! It's a stirring thought and a defining word — *conquerors*. We love that last verse. We say, "Yes! That's what I'm talking about!"

Of course, I always get just a little queasy reading the verse that comes just before that one: *As it is written: "For your sake we face death all day long; we are considered as sheep to be slaughtered."* Now, I'm just like the next parent; I love to think of my kids as conquerors for Christ. My heart does a flip, however, to think of

Gregg and Benjamin as sheep to be slaughtered. I want to say, "Wait a minute! Maybe I've got the wrong idea about what it means to be a conqueror." If I've got the wrong idea, I need to go back to the text and look at the fine print, if you will. Before I can help nurture my child to be a conqueror for Christ, I need to understand what that means to God. I need to understand, ultimately, what that's going to mean for me.

In All Things

Look at how the first verse of the passage, verse 28, starts: "*And we know that **in all things**....*"This passage starts and ends that way. Verse 37 says, "*No, **in all these things** we are more than conquerors through him who loved us*" (emphasis added). Okay, so what are these "things" we're supposed to know about? Well, I think they're the good and the bad, the ups and the downs, the yings and the yangs of life. I think they're the challenges life holds for your child and the protections God has to counter those challenges. I think "in all these things" is a way of saying "in life itself."

Isn't it comforting to know that God has already thought of everything? As a parent with two small children, and boys at that, every time my wife and I go anywhere with them, we have to act as expert prognosticators. Do they have their shoes? Their coats? Something to keep them occupied on the way? A favorite toy or game? We need to take into account where we're going, how long it's going to take to get there, how long we're going to be there, and what we might need for the boys as a consequence. When they were babies, it was even worse. No matter how prepared we thought we were, invariably we forgot something or overlooked some potential situation. In a similar way, we are heading out the door of life, with our children in tow, and there is just no way to think of everything! That's why it is great to know we don't have to. According to this passage, God's got it covered. No matter what happens, God's going to make sure it works out for good.

Do we really believe that? After all, we're talking about our kids here. As Christians, we understand that God is powerful, yet in our minds we often harbor the *what about* or *what if* thoughts.

Yes, God is powerful, but *what if* my child develops an illness? Or, yes, God is powerful, but *what about* the culture we live in? God is powerful but *what about* my own failings as a parent? *What if* the challenge is too great?

No matter how many *what abouts* or *what ifs*, God already has an answer and a solution. Let's look at the passage again. There are always going to be "things" that happen in our lives. *In all things* isn't the issue here; rather, it is the fact that *God works*. His working through our "things" has already been promised and planned for. God's power is manifest through His intervention and sovereignty over our "things." He has considered the *what abouts* and the *what ifs* and still works for your child's good and His purpose. He's got you and your child covered — covered in Christ. That helps me feel better about the slaughtered sheep part.

According to His Purpose

Our children are so vulnerable; we feel it daily. They are bombarded with ideas, opinions, situations, and circumstances that chip away at their innocence. As they get older, they weather this external maelstrom while coming face to face with their own human shortcomings. You are the parent and your child needs to look to you for strength and stability. How you view your child, therefore, is vital. You must consistently remind yourself and your changing child that God has called him or her to His purpose. There's a bigger picture, here, and your child is an integral part of it.

There are going to be times when it's hard to see how God can use your child. He'll seem too little. She'll seem too scattered. He'll seem too defiant. She'll seem too distracted. Fortunately — for all of us — God is in this for the long haul. He's not going to give up on His purpose for your child. Philippians 2:13 reminds us "for it is God who works in you to will and to act according to his good purpose." God not only has a purpose for your child picked out, but He is actively in the process of shaping your child to be ready and able to accomplish that purpose. Your child's identity as a champion of God comes directly from this purpose. If you doubt your child is a champion, it may be because you are unclear that he or she has a purpose. Even if you can't see it yet, or aren't sure what it is, never doubt there is a purpose. Your job is not to define the purpose; your job is to defend the promise.

God works; God wills; God acts. These are incredibly powerful statements. After all, God's working created the universe. God's will brings about redemption. God's actions move mountains. This *same power* is at work in *your child*. There will be times you doubt your child or you doubt yourself; don't doubt God. This champion has been called according to His purpose, and God is actively and willfully working toward that end. This is a powerful truth and a source of great hope for all parents. I know I will fail. My child will fail. But God never fails. In this rests my hope for my child.

According to His Process

Where my children are concerned, I like to call the shots. I insist on knowing who they're with, where they're going, and what they're doing. This isn't to say I'm not spontaneous, but where my kids are concerned, certain areas just have to be covered. Why? Because I love them and want to know they're going to be as safe as possible. God is no different. As this passage clearly shows, God has gone to great lengths to make sure our children are taken care of.

God *foreknew* your child, His champion. In other words, God's relationship with your child started before yours did. In fact, the very first relationship your child had with anyone wasn't with you, it was with God. Psalm 139 says that God knew your child from the moment of conception and was intimately involved in that process. Further, Romans 8 says that God *planned for* your child. It isn't just a static knowledge; it's an active work in progress. This champion's direction has already been established; this champion's arenas are already known.

Going one step further, God not only knew your child before you did, He planned for your child to be like Christ. He knew your child before you did and He had plans for your child before you did. His plans trump yours. As a parent, that can be difficult to accept (we'll talk more about that a little later) but it's true. God has *designs* on your child and has had those longer than it's possible for us to calculate. These are *eternal* designs and plans, carried out in the here and now.

Now, God doesn't just keep this relationship and these plans a secret. They may not be recognizable at the moment, but God is calling your child to them, even now. Since God created your child with his or her own unique championship tasks in mind, your child is created to respond to God's special call. This champion, your child, is designed to reverberate with that call. It will *resonate* with your child in a way that is unique to him or her.

God calls all of us; He invites us to be a part of His plans for us. Your child will have a choice we all have when called — answer, ignore, or refuse. When your child is called to make that choice, to whom will he or she go? Where will be the examples to emulate? As a parent, you want to be able to say to your child, "Look here! Look to me! This is how you answer the call." Notice, I didn't say this is what you answer; I said this is how you answer. It makes a difference, since your child's call will probably sound very different from yours. If you expect it to sound the same, you won't recognize it when it comes and you won't be able to point your child in the right direction. We need to ask ourselves, *Am I able to hear God's voice in my own walk? Am I able to recognize it and respond accordingly? If my child asks me what God sounds like, what would be my answer?*

Take heart, Romans 8:31 says, "What, then, shall we say in response to this? *If God is for us, who can be against us?*" God is on your side when you're on His side, when you're answering the call. (Even when you're not, He's still working on your behalf to bring you back to Him. This, of course, is also true of your child.) What that means for you as a parent is that you're not alone. Your child is not alone. There's a process going on here and God is in charge. That's good to know when it seems like you're sending your little lamb out among wolves.

We Are as Sheep

Back to the slaughtered sheep part. This is a reality that's difficult for us to accept as parents. We want to shield our children from the wolves of this world, as we should. The sad truth is, hard as we try, we can't keep our kids totally safe. Again, the world with its values intrudes. As a parent, you protect as much as you're able but trouble, hardship, and persecution will not veer away from your child. For many Christian parents, especially in some parts of this world, the famine, nakedness, danger, and sword talked about in Romans 8:35 are very real threats to the well-being of their children. My prayers go out to those parents. My gratitude goes out to God that I live in a society where I am able to feed, clothe, and, for the most part, protect my children.

This should not be used, however, to lull ourselves into a sense of false security. We need to realize the dangers present in this world, both physical and spiritual. Our job as parents is to protect our children as best we can, while teaching them how to protect themselves. We need to ask ourselves, *what blinders hinder me from recognizing the dangers threatening my child?* The terrible truth is, there are people and forces in the world and the heavenly realm that see your child as a sheep to be slaughtered. When this evil looks at Gregg or Benjamin, it does not see a beautiful soul to be loved and protected, it sees a potential victim to be devoured and destroyed. This is the evil I must protect my child against. It is the evil God is preparing my child to conquer.

More Than Conquerors

I'm not sure I would have the courage for the sheep part, if it wasn't for this assurance in verse 37: "No, in all these things we are more than conquerors through him who loved us." With the wolves out there, I need to know that even if my child is considered a sheep, he has a Good Shepherd on guard, watching over him, who loves him. This gives me hope and courage in parenting. This lets me know I'm not alone. No matter how hard I try, I can't protect my children from every danger. As a human being, I know that evil always wins the first round when it comes to our children; they will sin and fall short of the glory of God (that's a little earlier, in Romans 3:23.) I couldn't stop it in myself and I can't stop it for my children. I can prepare myself and my child for it.

The Story of Hannah: Where Rubber Meets the Road

God is molding my sons into champions for Him. We're all in my car — my life as a parent — but I'm not in the driver's seat, God is. I like to be in the driver's seat, especially when it's my car. My wife and I are blessed to each have a car. If we get ready to go somewhere and decide to take my car, I drive. I don't really like to take her car, because if we do, she drives. It feels wrong not to drive. It just seems odd not to be driving *my* car. I like to be in control. I'm a confident driver.

As good a driver as I am in my car, God's a better one when it comes to my life and the life of my family. That's easy to admit, but extremely difficult to put into practice. *It's my car, my kids, and I want to drive!* Even when I let God drive my car, I still find myself clutching the overhead handle around turns, stomping my foot on the floorboards if I think we should stop, and getting antsy if I think we're going too s -- l -- o -- w. All those things I hate in backseat drivers, I can easily do when God's driving my life. I'm even worse when my kids are in the car.

I need help to learn how to handle not being in control where my kids are concerned. How do I learn to trust God with the lives of my children? As in all things, God has anticipated my question. To help me — and you — He's provided a story in the Bible that's perfect for parents — the story of Hannah in the Old Testament Book of 1 Samuel. Here's a short synopsis. I'd encourage you to read the whole story yourself during a devotional time and make note of where God is speaking to you and your particular situation. This is a story for all parents but, by reading it over yourself, God can speak to you individually:

Hannah was one of two wives of Elkanah and she was unable to have children. Because of this, the other wife tormented her. Even though Hannah was loved by her husband, she was miserable as year after year, the harassment continued. Each year the whole household went to the temple in Jerusalem to sacrifice to the Lord. One year, Hannah made a pledge to God that if He would give her a son, she would turn him over to the Lord. At first, the priest at the temple,

Eli, thought Hannah was drunk because of the fervent way she was praying before God. After being assured she was deeply troubled, not drunk, Eli blessed her and the household returned home.

God remembered Hannah's prayer and granted her a son. In her joy, Hannah didn't forget where this child came from and even named him Samuel, which sounds like "heard of God." From the outset, she explained to Elkanah that Samuel belonged to the Lord and as soon as he was weaned, she was going to take him to the temple for service.

Hannah fulfilled her pledge and left her small son in the hands of complete and total strangers.

Okay, maybe that last part's a little provocative, but it's true. Hannah, with full understanding and the permission of her husband, essentially takes a very small child and leaves him at the temple. Granted, the second chapter of 1 Samuel goes on to say that the family got to visit Samuel once a year, but still, when Hannah said she would give the child over to the Lord, she wasn't kidding!

I'm not sure I have as much courage. I'm glad I'm not asked to give my child over to the Lord like that. Or, am I? Are you? What can we learn from Hannah? Here are a couple of things I've learned from thinking about this story, knowing God will reveal to you your own special insights.

Know where your children really come from. Hannah was very aware that God was the source of her child. Yes, he was the physical product of Hannah and Elkanah, but Samuel was ultimately a product of God's love and mercy to Hannah. The Scripture says God *remembered* Hannah and her prayer and allowed her to conceive a child.

Children come to us in a variety of ways. They are conceived by us, adopted, or fostered from others. For those of us who conceive children, I think it can be more difficult to really see the child as coming from God. We know this intellectually, but it's hard to separate out the fact when every time we look at him or her we see our own face, expression, or mannerism looking back at us. We see Grandma Ruth or Uncle John. We see a mother or father, a sister or brother. The strength of the physical origin can cause us to forget the spiritual origin.

In my life I've known several couples who experienced the joy of adopting or fostering a child. Often, these couples struggled for years to have children of their own, only to be unsuccessful. Their heartache was so evident and certainly felt by the members of their spiritual family. What absolute joy, then, when these couples were able to adopt or foster a new life into their family. The wait and the frustration produced a very real understanding and appreciation for the child as a gift from the Lord. Because the child did not come easily but was agonized over and prayed for, the answer of "Yes" from God was easier to be heard and remembered.

Hannah suffered for years. She waited and bore the brunt of unrelenting harassment from Elkanah's other wife, who had many children. She prayed and prayed for deliverance, for redemption from her childless state. Her conception of Samuel occurred after this ardent prayer. Hannah had no doubt where this child came from.

Gregg and Benjamin are an exquisite blending of people I've known and loved in my life. When I see them, I see myself, LaFon, our parents, and siblings. As beautiful as that is, it must not obscure the fact that Gregg and Bemjamin ultimately don't belong to me, they belong to God. Hannah understood this and so should I.

See your child as God's champion. Right from the beginning, Hannah understood that if God gave her a son, he was going to be special. In verse 11, Hannah promises that she will raise him to be special, to be set apart. She pledges to raise him to be a Nazirite. (This is where she says that no razor will touch his head. The other famous Nazirite in the Old Testament is Samson, and we'll talk about him in a later chapter!) I need to see my children, no matter their age, as special and set apart for God.

This can be hard for us as parents. After all, what parent wants their child to be different, to not fit in? If we were popular ourselves as kids, we might worry that our children won't experience the same level of acceptance. If we had trouble fitting in as kids, we may harbor a desire for our children to be popular because we weren't when growing up. It's not our child's job to either continue or rectify our own status as kids growing up. Being God's champion isn't a personality or popularity contest. It isn't about fitting in with the world. It's about standing up, not staying low. It's about being a beacon, not a blender.

Our children have been set apart by God; they are called out of the world. This will not win them a worldly popularity contest — quite the opposite. Jesus said in John 15:19: "If you belonged to the world, it would love you as its own. As it is, you do not belong to the world, but I have chosen you out of the world. That is why the world hates you." I venture to say that every Christian parent, at some point, has had to explain this difficult concept to an upset son or daughter. If your child is going to be different from those around him or her, isn't it better to be a champion? For your child to view him or herself as that champion, you need to see it yourself.

Keep your pledges before the Lord concerning your children. Have you ever prayed one of those *If only A, then B* prayers? If only you'll do A for me, God, then I'll do B for you? If only you'll do what I want, then I'll do what you want, is basically what these prayers boil down to. They're often said in times of extreme desperation. Does this type of prayer seem manipulative or wrong to you? It didn't to Hannah. Hers is a classic *If A, then B* desperation prayer: *If You'll give me a child, God, I'll give him back to You.*

It's not really that remarkable that Hannah made this type of prayer. After all, she was fairly desperate and pretty fed up with the treatment of Elkanah's other wife. What is remarkable is that she kept it. How often do we send up this kind of prayer, only to back out of the deal when God delivers? Not Hannah. She made the pledge and kept it, even though most of us as parents would find it excruciating to be separated from our children, especially at a young age. Hannah believed enough in God to make the prayer and she believed enough in God to keep the prayer. Hers was a two-part faith that I need to have. I need to have faith enough to ask, and when God delivers, I need to have faith that it really is Him working in my life and keep my part of the deal. After all, my prayer is a verbal contract with God.

What this means to me is I need to honor my pledges. If I have pledged to teach my children about God, I need to take that seriously.

Gregg and Benjamin need to know more about God than they do about soccer or superheroes. Not that these other things are bad, but my priority needs to be God. My practice also needs to honor my pledges. If I've promised to teach my children to know, honor, and love God, then I need to know, honor, and love God myself. Who is my child's first teacher? I am. My life speaks louder than my words, so both had better be as unified as possible.

Don't keep your vision for your child a secret. From the very beginning, Hannah made sure her husband understood about her vision for Samuel. She didn't try to hide it, but actively secured his permission. When she tells Elkanah about her rather radical plan to drop their only son off at a distant religious institution, he says the words I'm sure all wives would love to hear: *Do what seems best to you.* It's a testimony to Hannah's life that Elkanah had this level of faith in her. When it is time to fulfill Hannah's vow, the two of them go together to present Samuel as well as an offering to the Lord. It may have started as Hannah's pledge, but it became a joint vision they shared for their son. I cannot help but believe that this — more than anything else — strengthened their relationship with God and their relationship with each other.

Give God glory for what He will do through your child. What's interesting to me is the timing of when Hannah sings her song of praise to God. You'd think it would be after she realizes she's conceived a child or after giving birth. Instead, her outpouring of joy to God is expressed not when she is given the child but when she gives the child up. This outpouring of praise to and faith in God is a beautiful song found in I Samuel 2:1–10, that reminds me of the song Mary, the mother of Jesus, sings in Luke 1:46–55. Hannah got it. She recognized that God is a fulfiller of promises and would work His will in her son. Knowing that, she could let him go and sing praise. What a powerful lesson for me, as a parent.

Recognize God's blessings in your life through your faithfulness. God appreciates what we give up in this life to follow Him. He is a rewarder of faithfulness. Because Hannah was faithful to her pledge and trusted God to take care of her only child, God gave her five more — three sons and two daughters. He filled up the void in her life created when Samuel went to live in the temple. Jesus promises us the same thing in Mark 10:29–30: "I tell you the truth," Jesus replied, "no one who has left home or brothers or sisters or mother or father or children or fields for me and the gospel will fail to receive a hundred times as much in the present age (homes, brothers, sisters, mothers, children and fields — and with them, persecutions) and in the age to come, eternal life." God will bless you in this life for the sacrifices you make, including giving up your child to His care. This is not a sugar-coated, Santa-like promise; Jesus in His honesty and wisdom cautions that with the promise come persecutions — oh, and eternal life.

Accepting God's Arenas

Yes, for much of your child's life, you are in the driver's seat. You set the rules and you determine the outcome. However, for your child to truly become God's champion, there's a time when you must let go and accept a supporting role in your child's future, even if God takes the car, with your child in it, to places you wouldn't go if you were the driver. As God's champion, your child may enter arenas you never would have chosen for him or her.

Arenas often mean battles. It's tough to think about your child engaged in battle, but without the battle, there's no champion. Your child, God's champion, will need to undergo the crucible of battle in order to be prepared to conquer. In truth, our children fight battles all the time. As Christians, they are raised within a faith structure that is misunderstood by many and openly despised by some. As they grow, they will undergo those inner battles all of us face. (I think these are probably some of the hardest for parents to weather.) When we see our child in the midst of a battle, our initial reaction is often to yank them out, thinking it's too hard. Sometimes, God wants our child right where he or she is, in the heart of the battle. Our job isn't to tell them to run away, but to support them and help them to stand firm in the Lord.

Battles can be tremendous faith builders and produce unprecedented times of family unity and solidarity. We need to teach our children how to avoid unnecessary conflict but there are times when the standard must be raised and a stand must be taken. Perhaps it's when your child is criticized for his Christian beliefs or confronted about her stand on controversial issues. These are times when your child is tested and, handled well, strengthened.

As a parent, it's not up to us to control every arena our child enters, any more than it's possible for us to shield our children from all hurt or pain. We want our children to learn to ride bikes, to run and play, even if it means a stubbed toe or a sprained ankle. We want them to make friends with other children, even though it means they will eventually be called a name or treated unfairly. These things hurt but they are part of life, and our children need to learn how to deal with life, not run from it. In a similar way, God may choose to put our children in a difficult family situation or school environment in order to further the process of molding His champion.

It's amazing how perceptive children can be. They are able to take their "child-sized" circumstances and apply spiritual applications. God is very real to them and they are alert to His working in their world. After all, we tell them that God loves them and is looking over them. They fully expect Him to be involved in what happens to them. How do we know this? By listening in on the conversations our children have with God through their prayers. Children are very honest in prayer and ask God for help in all kinds of situations. It is only as we get older that we learn "prayer language" and lose the spontaneity and familial closeness we had with God when we were younger. In fact, as adults we often spend a great deal of time trying to get back to that simpler time when we were kids, just talking to God.

Because God is very real to children, we need to honor that faith. We must teach our children not to avoid all struggles but remind them that God is in the midst of their struggles. Our children need to experience God in the midst of their struggles. Shielding our children from all struggles shields them from seeing God at work. It prevents them from learning how to cope with adversity. How can our children learn to get up if we never allow them to fall down? How can our children be champions if we keep yanking them out of the arena?

Taking the Back Seat

Are you prepared for your child to surpass you spiritually? Are you ready for your child to go and do more for God than you have? Can you allow your child's faith to teach you more about your own? As parents, we can feel proprietary about our children's faith. It should look like ours, agree with ours. What if it's different from ours? What if it's bigger than ours?

As you prepare God's champion, be aware of your own reactions to his or her growing faith. This faith will not look like yours in many ways. This can be comforting and scary, all at the same time. It's comforting to know that God can propel our children further than our own spiritual momentum. It's scary, though, to see them speeding across the spiritual planes, headed to God-knows-where. We've got to be ready to let them soar on God's wings. Our job is to help prepare them for the journey, not dictate to God the flight plan.

Daily Devotion

Parenting my children is the hardest task I've ever endeavored. Daily I'm confronted with my own shortcomings, and I thank God for these reminders. It helps me to remember to get on my knees and give myself — as well as my children — over to God. In so much of my personal and professional life, I feel in control. I've set my priorities and made plans. I know (for the most part) where I'll be each day and what I'll be doing. This can create an illusion of control that's very seductive. It's easy for me to think, *I've done this. I'm in charge. I'm in the driver's seat.* Being a parent, however, has forced me to learn just how much is beyond my manipulation! I deeply desire my children to be happy, healthy, and godly, but it seems I'm so often swimming furiously against the tide of this life and my own shortcomings.

In order to cope with this constant uncertainty, I grasp even more tightly to God. Here's how I prepare myself each day. I offer these to you, not to say, "See how pious I am," but as one parent to another.

I turn each day over to God. As the founder of the Center for Counseling and Health Resources, a large Christian-based counseling agency, I'm "in charge." I make decisions, large and small, every day that affect many lives — those of my family, those of my staff, those of our clients. As a father, it's natural for me to think of myself as "in charge" of my household. This is a trap that I must daily resist. God is in charge of my household, through me. If God is not in charge of me, He is not in charge of my household. I love my family too much to let that happen. Through prayer and willful submission, I consciously strive to allow God to be in charge. I ask for His guidance when making decisions. With eyes of faith, I look for Him at work in my world. I want to be alert to what He's doing so I make sure I'm "on board." The reason I have to be so intentional about it is because it's so hard! I can be as short-sighted and stubborn as the next person. So I work to keep God in the forefront of my mind and my life. It's a battle of wills and I need God in order to win, for my business, my family, and myself.

I turn my children over to God. I love my children so much I want to keep them close. Keeping them close can mean keeping them within my control. In a broader sense, this is prudent as a parent and part of my job. But spiritually, I need to turn my children daily over to God, to allow Him to do what is necessary to mold them into His champions. Again, I need to allow God to place my children in arenas I would not choose myself. As hard as it is to turn myself over to God, it's geometrically harder to turn my children over to God. *Which is why I have to commit to it daily.*

I daily renew my commitment to be faithful to the mother of my children. Someone once said that the best gift I can give my children is to love their mother. By upholding my vow to LaFon, I teach my children how to keep their own vows. By upholding my vow to LaFon, I do everything in my power to ensure my marriage stays strong for my children. Study after study has shown that kids do better in a stable, intact home. I understand the pain of divorce, and it's not my intention to cause those of you who are divorced to feel guilty about that decision. My point and my plea is for those of us who are married to stay that way, whenever and however possible. If your marriage relationship is rocky, it's going to cause those foundations for your champion to totter. We used to tell people to stay together "for the sake of the children." This is always my preference and something we work very hard to do at the Center — reconcile husbands and wives back to each other, for the sake of their children, as well as for their own.

I stay close to God myself so I can show my children the way. My child may be the champion but I'm one of the primary trainers. That means I need to be spiritually fit myself. Just like physical exercise, I need to work out spiritually each day, in prayer, meditation, and study of the Word. It's hard to find a quiet time during the day to stay spiritually fit, but I do it by getting into work very early in the morning. There, before the business gets up and running, I get up and running spiritually by engaging in at least an hour of personal quiet time with God.

You don't have to do it the same way I do, but I encourage you to find a consistent time with a goal of daily observance. Things happen — that's just part of life, but the goal is to spend time each day in spiritual communion. The only way I've ever found to make this work is to set aside a set time each day when I don't allow anything but an emergency to intrude.

Include prayer, meditation, and examining the Word as part of your quiet time. Spend time with God, get to know Him, learn to hear His voice. The groundwork you lay in your own life is the foundation of faith for your family.

Training Ground

So many thoughts swirl in our minds when we think of all we hope and desire for our children. As hard as it is to corral those thoughts, I'd like you to take a moment and do just that. First, write down the hopes you have for your children. This doesn't need to be long — just a sentence or phrase that captures each desire. Next, turn your child over to God in writing. Acknowledge in your pledge that it is God who controls the life of your child. Lastly (and don't leave this part out!), do like Hannah and write down your praise to God for all that He has done in your life. Hannah had confidence that God would take care of Samuel because she personally experienced His love and grace in her own life.

When you have written these three parts, say them as a prayer to God. If you're like me, you'll need to say them often, certainly more than once, as you fortify yourself to raise God's champion, your child. Your child is in training and so are you. It's part of our role as parent to this incredible gift from God. Mine are named Gregg and Benjamin. Make a personal pledge and prayer for each of yours.

If you have difficulty expressing your thoughts, don't give up! In the last chapter, you'll find information on *The Power of a Praying Parent* by Stormie Omartian. I have found great comfort in praying these prayers for my children. They are specifically set up to do this easily. If you're having trouble putting your own prayers to words, pick up this book or another like it and claim the prayers of others. You can also read through Scripture and claim that promise for your child.

In order to help you, here's one I've prayed, taken from Stormie's book, on page 141:

> *Lord, I pray that Gregg will so love the Lord with all his heart, soul, and mind that there will be no room in him for the lies of the enemy or the clamoring of the world. May the Word of God take root in his heart and fill his mind with things that are true noble, just, pure, lovely, of good report, virtuous, and praiseworthy. Give him understanding that what goes into his mind becomes part of him, so that he will weigh carefully what he sees and hears.*

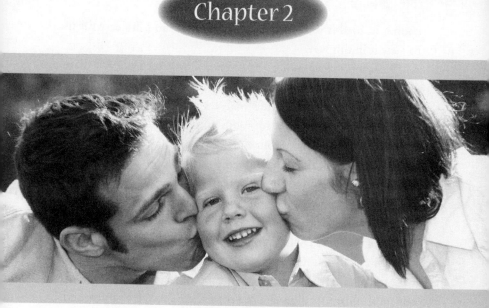

Chapter 2

Preparing
Your Family

But as for me and my household, we will serve the LORD (Josh. 24:15).

Many of us who belong to a faith community refer to it as *the family of God*. We call our fellow believers brothers and sisters in Christ. Peter calls us the family of God in 1 Peter 4:17. The New Testament is replete with examples of this familial form of address. Many of us take Jesus' promise in Mark 10:28–29 (that we talked about in the previous chapter) to be speaking of the mothers, fathers, sisters, and brothers we gain in the church, who are often closer to us physically, emotionally, and spiritually than our biological family. The local congregation or the church in total is recognized as the family of God. It's easy for us to view it in this way.

Now, what about our own families? Do we see our immediate family unit as a family of God? Just as the local congregation is a place for God's people to grow and develop, so is our immediate family. It's important not to compartmentalize our religion by thinking that the church is our spiritual family and our actual family is merely physical. LaFon, Gregg, and Benjamin are no less my spiritual family than the church we attend.

The family is a vital component in the molding of a champion. It's not just me and Gregg — God's champion. It's not just me and Benjamin — God's champion. Instead, it's me, LaFon, Gregg, and Benjamin — all of us God's champions. Realistically, then, does that make too many champions under one roof? After all, it takes a lot of work and effort to mold a champion. Is there enough to go around with multiple champions all drawing from the same family?

If the resources were being exclusively drawn from that family, I'd venture to say "No." Just look at the families of, say, Olympic athletes. All of the family time, energy, resources, and money are often funneled into furthering the prospects of that one future Olympian. Deep sacrifices are made by parents and, unfortunately for some, required by siblings. It's similar in any household where one family member is given the bulk of the attention. The family is stretched thin, to the point of breaking, sadly in some cases, due to the pressure.

In the family of God that exists under my roof, however, the resources needed to mold our champions does not come exclusively from within. Rather, the resources are being drawn from God, who has infinitely more to give than just the human efforts of any one of us or even all of us collectively. God is able to empower and provide for all of His champions living under my roof.

That is, of course, if I move out of the way and let God lead my family. Family done right gives all members strength and encouragement to live out their God-ordained purpose. Family done wrong creates strife, animosity, and jealousy.

Family Done Wrong

From Genesis, we know that God created individuals and he created family (Gen. 2:24). Family happens fairly quickly in the timeline of events. Family problems also surface in short order. Blame and lying trip up Adam and Eve, resulting in expulsion from the Garden. Jealously rears its ugly head between Cain and Abel, resulting in Abel's murder. Later on, in Genesis 27, we read of the jealousy between Esau and Jacob, the sons of Isaac. Now, with this fraternal jealousy, Esau did not kill Jacob, but their brotherly love and relationship effectively died and would not be rekindled for many years after being apart.

God meant for family to bring people together. Sin, however, forces families apart. As parents, we must be aware of the sin happening, inevitably, in our own families. This sin, left unconfessed and uncontained, will also certainly mold and shape our children, to their detriment. It is not possible for us to remain sinless within our families but we need to be sensitive to our sin and continually bring it before each other and the Lord, asking for strength and forgiveness.

With Cain and Abel, and Esau and Jacob, the jealousy and animosity that existed stemmed from birth order. This can be true in families today. The firstborn child, even in our culture, has status within the family. Arriving into the family first, it can be natural to see him or her as the leader. First in birth, first in everything. As is so often the case, however, God may see things very differently. He doesn't judge value by birth order. His plans are not defined by who comes first. On the contrary, God often mixes up conventional wisdom by changing the apparent order of things. Think, for example, of *"the first shall be last and the last shall be first"* as expressed by Jesus in places like Matthew 20:16, Mark 10:31, and Luke 13:30. I believe this is God reminding us that He is sovereign and not to trust our human tendency to place value in the wrong places.

Cain may have had more status within his human family because of being the first-born son, but God judged on his actions; his offering to God was not acceptable when Abel's was. How does this apply to the champions under our roof? We must not place more emphasis on the older champion, to the detriment of other, younger children. God will have battles and victories for each child. We must not allow human value judgments to impede our vision of the possible with our children. God has mixed things up in other families; He may very well do the same in ours.

What happens, then, if it appears God has favored a younger child more than an older child? If you're molding more than one champion, don't fall into the trap of giving preference to one over the other — neither the older nor the younger. This is favoritism and it never leads to healthy results for anyone involved.

Let's take a look at the problem favoritism played in the lives of Isaac's family, found in the later part of the Book of Genesis. Our cast of characters includes Isaac, certainly a champion for God in his own right, Rebekah, his wife, and Esau and Jacob, their twin sons. Being twins, you'd think they'd have equal status, but Esau was born first and therefore was entitled to the birthright of first born. This wasn't just a descriptor back in those days, but carried with it a great deal of cultural significance, including status in the family and rights of inheritance. (For a wonderful and important book outlining this story and its familial consequences in depth, I heartily recommend Gary Smalley and John Trent's book, *The Blessing*, included in the last chapter of this book.)

This was a family divided. Esau, the first-born twin, was favored by Isaac, and Jacob, the second-born twin, was favored by Rebekah. It's difficult to know all of the reasons but, as is often the case, each parent was drawn more to the child most like themselves. Isaac loved to hunt and eat wild game and so did Esau. The two understood each other and liked to do the same things. Jacob, on the other hand, was quiet and liked to stay around home, nearer to Rebekah. The two of them were close and spent more time together. Instead of each parent recognizing their own natural affinity toward one of their twins and therefore working more diligently to get to know and interact with the other, Isaac and Rebekah picked their favorites and left it at that.

Actually, they did a little more than just leave it at that. Each parent began to actively intervene on behalf of the favored child. Granted, God did reveal that Esau would serve Jacob prior to the twins being born, but this was a prophecy regarding not just the boys but the nations they would come to represent. When the time came for Isaac to give a blessing to his sons prior to his death, his plans were different than God's. Even though, through Rebekah's deception, Isaac was actually speaking to Jacob, he thought it was Esau he was blessing, in direct contradiction to what God had foretold. (If this all seems a fairly complicated plot, I encourage you to read the whole story in Genesis 25–33.) As parents, we must not fall into the trap of favoring one of our children above another.

This favoritism, even without official birthrights, is still wrong. In order to prepare the family unit to mold champions, each child should feel valued and special by both parents. (This is true even when the parents no longer live together.) When favoritism exists, children will often disregard the favor of one parent and focus on the disregard of the other, as proof of their unworthiness. Instead of devoting themselves to God's purpose, they may harness all their energies to gain the approval of the distant or disapproving parent. They become the champion of the dissatisfied parent, who may never acknowledge that child's value. Detoured from their affirming purpose in God, they wander hopelessly off, spinning their wheels like a rodent in a cage, chasing after an illusive affirmation that never comes. This is a life derailed and a champion defeated.

God's Big Tent

God doesn't show partiality (Deut. 10:17). God goes all-out in providing for his spiritual family, even to the point of giving up His only son, Jesus. Listen again to our Romans 8 passage, where verse 32 says: *"He who did not spare his own Son, but gave him up for us all — how will he not also, along with him, graciously give us all things?"* God did not give Jesus for just one of your children. He does not favor one of your children over another. He does not love one of your children more than another. He does not have better plans for one over another. His plans, undoubtedly, will be different for each child, but He is not partial. As parents, we must emulate God's even-handed love.

As we've seen in the story of Isaac, this can be difficult to do, especially when we have a natural affinity for one child over the other. It could simply be because of gender. It could be because of temperament, personality, or aptitude. As a parent, I encourage you to pray and search your heart for any hint of favoritism or partiality. Ask your spouse or other close adults to evaluate your interactions with your children. Ask your children if they think they're being treated unfairly in any way. If one child feels marginalized, it's important for you to know about it. Be willing to listen to the feedback from your children. If your children sense there is a comparison being made, they will feel a sense of competition with siblings. Rather than learn to value and appreciate who they are, they will begin to envy and desire to be like someone else. This is not a healthy situation for God's champion, who must come to grips with who he or she is in the Lord, in order to embrace their unique, God-given destiny.

Realize you could be dealing with an actual situation of favoritism or it could be a matter of perception. An older child may feel a younger child is coddled. A younger child may feel an older child is more "privileged." Instead of trying to justify or explain away the feeling, listen to your child. Ask for examples of when he or she saw this happening. Be open to making changes in how you interact with your children accordingly. If it is a matter of perception (for example the older child doesn't understand a younger child is not expected to perform at the same level or the younger child doesn't understand an older age means more privileges), it's no less important for you to work with your child to view the situation differently. This is imperative for family unity and cohesion. We want the whole family cheering on the sidelines when one of us conquers for Christ, not pouting on the sidelines, silently angry and jealous, feeling even more marginalized and resentful.

Family Done Right

Because of the adversarial nature of their relationship growing up, Esau and Jacob lived a good portion of their lives separated from each other. Needless to say, after Jacob stole the birthright, Esau was less than pleased, even though he'd basically bartered it away for a meal earlier in his life. In fact, Genesis 27:41 says that Esau was mad enough to make plans to kill Jacob. Rebekah, naturally, intervened and sent Jacob to live apart until Esau's anger faded, and live apart they did for many years.

Now, it might seem, reading through Genesis, that there aren't any siblings who were able to rise up as champions for God and still speak to each other! Happily for us, though, the Book of Genesis is followed by the Book of Exodus, which details a family that was able to be champions for God and still stay together. This is the story of a sister and her two younger brothers — Miriam, Moses, and Aaron. This family had a rocky start. You'll remember that Moses was born during a time when Pharaoh in Egypt had given a decree to kill all the male Hebrew children. Moses' mother hid him for three months after birth, but when she just couldn't hide him any longer she covered a basket with tar, placed Moses in the basket, and floated it off down the Nile River. His older sister Miriam watched from a distance to see what would happen to her baby brother. Well, God had plans for this baby and the whole family.

Yes, it was God's plan for Moses to be His champion, to rescue the people of Israel from oppressive Egyptian slavery. His plans didn't leave out Miriam, Moses' sister, for Scripture tells us that she was a prophetess (Exod. 15:20), nor did they leave out Moses' brother Aaron who was a Levite and chosen by God to act as Moses' spokesman. This family was full of mighty, empowered champions for God, yet they were able to stay together and work together to accomplish God's purposes.

It is normal for different children to have separate interests, strengths, and abilities. That's what makes us unique individuals. We're not supposed to like the same things or do the same things or be good at the same things, but even within a diverse family like

Moses', God worked the pieces together to create a whole. This is what I strive for in my own family. It's not necessary for each of us to be identical. Frankly, I enjoy the variety! What we are unified about is our commitment to God, whatever that looks like and wherever that takes us.

I am no less a champion myself when I'm on the sidelines rooting for LaFon or one of the boys. Their victories do not diminish my own. I want my boys to strive individually to be the best they can be for God. I also want them to cheer on and encourage each other to do the same. I want my boys to be like Miriam, Moses, and Aaron.

I also want my boys to be like Philip, in the New Testament, who included his brother in the most significant events of his life. When Philip met Jesus, his first inclination wasn't to keep this incredible event to himself. Now, if this were Cain or Esau, I'm afraid each might have wanted to keep something so significant all to himself, but not Philip. He went right away, ran even, to find his brother Nathanael. Philip was more than happy to make his love for Jesus "a family affair."

Now Jesus actually called a number of families to join Him, not just Philip and Nathanael. Andrew and Simon, who was also known as Peter, met Jesus together and followed Him together. James and John, the sons of Zebedee, did likewise. That's how I want my boys to be. When one of them "meets Jesus" in whatever form that takes, I want him to run to find the other, to share the blessing. It is within the context of family that children learn what it means to be a blessing to others and to be blessed by others. If jealousy, envy, or favoritism is present, this opportunity is lost.

Families need to literally run to share blessings with each other. We need to share and not hoard. We need to be able to talk about what's happening in our lives spiritually and gain encouragement, strength, and support from those closest to us. When Abel was blessed by God, Cain became so jealous he murdered him. When Jacob was blessed by God through Isaac, Esau became so enraged that Jacob had to leave in order to be safe. When Philip was blessed by God, the first thing he did was run to get his brother. That's family done right.

The Household of Faith

For most of us, our families include not only our immediate spouse and siblings but also brothers, sisters, nieces, nephews, cousins, parents, aunts, and uncles. Even if these family members live far from us, they are nonetheless part of our extended family and have a role to play in molding a champion, for each of these people who interact with your child impart their own opinions, observations, and views about that child. The more they interact, the greater their influence. For this reason, your budding champion needs to be surrounded by family who supports God's purpose for your child. When this happens, their voices added to yours create an encouraging choir operating in harmony. When this doesn't happen, it can sound like a cacophony of mixed messages undermining your child's belief in him or herself, and even in God.

So must all family members be on the same page, spiritually? If not, does this automatically mean your child is hampered from becoming a spiritual champion? The answer, of course, is "no." Let's go again to the New Testament where we can look at the example of Timothy, in the Book of Acts. This book outlines the start of the early church, especially the conversion and missionary journeys of the apostle Paul. In Acts 16:1, Paul meets a disciple in the city of Lystra named Timothy. Timothy's mother was a Jew but his father was a Greek. Concerned about your own family? Look at this one! Realize this was not a family united in an understanding of God's purposes and plans. Even with a divided family — culturally and religiously — Timothy still had faith in God and became part of God's plan to spread the gospel to the world. That's a pretty big champion! God's plans are big enough to work around our obstacles.

Timothy's assets in his molding are not only his mother, Eunice, but also his grandmother, Lois. Timothy's mother had a choice in how she raised Timothy. She could have raised him according to the culture of his father, to be a Gentile. Instead, she molded him to be God's champion by making sure Timothy knew and loved God. Eunice enlisted the aid of her own mother, Lois, in this effort. Paul, in 2 Timothy 1:5, says, "I have been reminded of your sincere faith, which first lived in your grandmother Lois and in your mother Eunice and, I am persuaded, now lives in you also." Paul talks here about a *living* faith, not a passed-down, hereditary, obligatory faith but a living, breathing, active faith — the faith of a champion.

As you enlist the aid of your own extended family in molding the hearts and minds of your children, make sure they are surrounded by people who believe in them, who believe God has a purpose just for them, who picture a positive future for your children. It would be wonderful if every member of your extended family was a mature, enthusiastic believer, for the living faith of this extended family will breathe life into your child. I've seen this in my own life. The faith I have was first seen in my grandparents — O.J. and Maxine, Harry and Ruby — and in my parents, Larry and Judy. Unlike Timothy, it's active and alive in my wife, LaFon, and I'm passing it down to my sons, Gregg and Benjamin.

Preparing Your Family

What do you do, however, if family members aren't believers or have no faith of their own? You prepare your family by choosing it. Give your child the gift of spiritual grandparents, aunts, uncles, cousins. These are found where we started this chapter — in the church, the family of God. If you are not part of a local congregation, I urge you to find one. It's vital for your own spiritual walk and for your child. There, you'll be able to find Eunices and Loises, to mentor and love your child. Often, these are found in the garb of a Sunday school teacher or children's ministry worker. They can be young or old, male or female. Whichever, each will value your child and join wholeheartedly in God's special purpose for that child. They will view your child through the eyes of faith and see the future champion waiting to be unleashed for the Lord.

Does this mean that your child should have no interaction with members of your family who are not believers? Of course not! As

Christians, we are to be light to the world! The faith of your children is a powerful witness for God, especially for family members who do not yet know the Lord. As your child grows in faith, he or she will become aware of beloved family members who do not share or practice faith. This is not a reason to isolate; this is an opportunity for prayer. Allow your child to intercede for loved ones, to ask God to bless their lives and to increase their faith.

At this point, I must give an unfortunate word of caution. If you have family members who are openly hostile to your faith or who refuse to respect the way in which you are bringing up your child, or who act in an inappropriate or abusive manner, you have no choice but to separate from them, as much as possible. Your child should not be subjected to verbal harassment, threats, or ridicule because of faith in God. This is an arena for a full-fledged champion of God and your child may one day be called to defend their faith to extended family members. While they are small and growing, you will need to exercise your right and duty of a parent to protect your child from abusive or harmful situations.

Unhappily, for some of you, the abusive family you must protect your children against are your own parents. My heart goes out to you and I urge you, for the sake of your children, to complete the process of healing and recovery from this difficult situation. It can be hard for you to decide what is best for your children in this situation if you never have come to grips with what's best for yourself. It will not bless your children if you place them into the same abusive, negative relationships you grew up with as a child yourself. (As a springboard to healing and discovery, I urge you to read my book, *Healing the Scars of Emotional Abuse*. It's listed in the last chapter and many people have been able to work through painful family situations and memories, for their own sakes and for their children.)

A House Divided

This situation can be made even more difficult and distressing if the immediate family is divided — if, as a mother, the father doesn't believe, or if, as a father, the mother doesn't believe. This is a house divided, but take heart, so was Timothy's. If you are in a marriage or child situation where the other parent or spouse does not share your faith in God, I suggest the following:.

- Look for commonality wherever you can. A non-believing parent may still understand the benefit of a moral upbringing, stressing personal responsibility, honor, virtue, compassion. Seek common ground whenever possible.

- Recognize that your partner in raising your champion is God himself. Spouses who agree in faith understand this also, of course, but this will be a clear reality for you. You must ask God to strengthen you and equip you to mold your champion without the benefit of his or her other parent.

- Be a witness to your child of the value of faith. Ask yourself, *how do my actions show that faith makes a difference in my life?* If your reactions, attitudes, words, and actions show little difference from the non-believing parent, how will this speak to the transforming power of Christ? Allow your child to see faith in action through the way you conduct yourself in this situation.

- Avoid denigrating the other parent. Rather, explain clearly your views, your faith, your reasons for living the way you do. Allow your child to draw his or her own conclusions. Remember, children are predisposed to love their parents, even when those parents don't love each other. If you seek to hurt the other parent by the way you speak about him or her in front of the children, you're also injuring your child.

- Pray that God will use your situation to reveal himself to your child. There are so many spiritual corollaries to the earthly circumstances we find ourselves in. God is able to use your family situation to teach your child vital spiritual lessons. It may be these spiritual lessons that are molding your child into the very champion God intends. Trust Him to redeem a difficult family situation.

- Take advantage of every believer in your immediate and extended family, then look to the spiritual family of God to fill in the gaps. Prepare your child's family to embrace his or her future as a champion for God.

Training Ground

I'd like you to take an inventory of your family — biological and spiritual. Who is your child's extended family? Who operates as aunts, uncles, grandparents, siblings, cousins? Where are the holes? Whom could you see filling those holes? Ask yourself:

- Is my child surrounded by people who love and care about him or her?

- If my child can't be with me, who does he or she want to spend time with?

- Who does my child spend time with? Is this person a positive influence on my child?

- Does my child spend the majority of his or her time with people who love and have faith in God?

- Besides me, who else has the most influence over how my child thinks about the world and views him or herself?

Look over this information and spend time specifically in prayer that God will reveal to you those people He has placed in your child's life. Ask Him to confirm the people already in relationship with your child. Seek the wisdom to know if any changes need to be made and the courage to make those changes.

Father, as the creator of the family, I trust You with mine. I thank You for the special people you have already placed in my life and in the life of my child. Help me to see the gaps that exist in my family. I recognize that family relationships affect my child's family relationships. If there are relationships I need to mend, so those individuals can have a deeper role in the molding of my child, Your champion, help me to know that, help me to do that. If there are people I need to withdraw from in order to do what's best for my child, give me strength! Open my eyes to see the extended family, both biological and spiritual, which You have chosen to nurture my child to be Your champion.

Chapter 3

Preparing
Your Child

Finally, be strong in the Lord and in his mighty power. Put on the full armor of God so that you can take your stand against the devil's schemes. For our struggle is not against flesh and blood, but against the rulers, against the authorities, against the powers of this dark world and against the spiritual forces of evil in the heavenly realms. Therefore put on the full armor of God, so that when the day of evil comes, you may be able to stand your ground, and after you have done everything, to stand. Stand firm then, with the belt of truth buckled around your waist, with the breastplate of righteousness in place, and with your feet fitted with the readiness that comes from the gospel of peace. In addition to this, take up the shield of faith, with which you can extinguish all the flaming arrows of the

evil one. Take the helmet of salvation and the sword of the
Spirit, which is the word of God. And pray in the Spirit on
all occasions with all kinds of prayers and requests. With this
in mind, be alert and always keep on praying for all the saints
(Eph. 6:10–18).

There are times I wish I could encase my kids in one of those bubble suits and protect them from the world. You know the ones I'm talking about — they're made of transparent plastic and are meant to protect those with compromised immune systems. They have special ventilation to keep out germs; their outer layer of see-through plastic is puffed up with air to cushion any unexpected fall or bump. They allow the person inside to see the world outside, while still being protected from it. I know I can't do this literally, but I'd sure like to do it figuratively. I'd like to allow my kids to *experience* the world without the world *affecting* them.

I recognize, of course, that this isn't possible. My kids need to experience the world, be affected by the world, in order for the world to be affected *by them.* My children, God's champions, are meant to affect the world, and they can't do that in a bubble suit, but they can be protected while they're affecting the world. God has designed a special type of suit that doesn't involve plastic. Instead, it's a suit fit for a champion — a suit of armor to be exact and it's found in Ephesians 6:10–18. Unlike the bubble suit that keeps you safe *from* the world, this armor keeps you safe *in* the world.

Gearing Up

I guess you could say these are marching orders for God's champions — how we're supposed to gear up and head out. As such, I don't think they're meant for mature, adult Christians only. The spiritual battles we face in this life are not held in abeyance until the age of majority. Our children are daily in the fray, no matter what we do to shield them from it. God, in this passage, is telling us not to shield our children *from* the battle but equip our children *for* the battle. Armor is both defensive and offensive; it protects and equips.

Let's take a look at this passage, verse by verse, and see what God says about His chosen armor. Each component is not random, but carefully coordinated to provide our children with the protection they need and the resources God has marshaled on their behalf.

Finally, be strong in the Lord and in His mighty power. Before our children head into battle, they need to be grounded in the understanding that God and His power are on their side and available to them. This is a statement, not a suggestion. In fact, it's a command — a champion's command. Difficult, challenging situations can appear overwhelming, especially to children, who lack the longevity of experience to factor seemingly impossible odds. Our kids need to know that God is bigger than our circumstances, that His power is greater than that arrayed against them. From this understanding comes hope. From hope comes courage. From courage comes faith in action. From faith in action comes wisdom.

It is possible for our children to grow in wisdom. Luke 2:52 says that, as a child, Jesus grew in wisdom. Was this solely because He was God's Son? I don't believe so. I believe children have the inherent ability to understand God and grow in their knowledge of Him. Jesus isn't our exception, He's our example. Children are able to make spiritual connections and grow. How do I know this? I know it because of Christ's example and my own personal experience with Gregg and Benjamin.

One day, without prompting, Gregg bowed his head, folded his hands and began to pray. He said, "Thank you, God, for everyone. The good guys and the bad guys. We don't like what the bad guys do but we love them." I don't know what prompted the prayer, what "bad guys" he was talking about, but I do know the outcome of the prayer — Gregg was growing in wisdom.

Even Benjamin, at three, knows who God is and responds to what he's learning from me and LaFon, from his older brother Gregg, and from church. It isn't just knowledge he's gaining, it's also wisdom. **I will help my children know that a mighty God is their source of strength.**

Put on the full armor of God so that you can take your stand against the devil's schemes. Our kids will be called upon to stand up against all kinds of evil — prejudice, injustice, envy, jealousy. They will need to stand up for themselves; they will be called upon to stand up for others. Unfortunately, I don't get to control when and where my children will be called upon to stand up and be counted for God. The more my children interact with the world around them, the more likely it is they will face situations that require them to stand up for what is right. As adults, we recognize that when you stand up for what's right, it can feel like you're up there by yourself with a big target on your chest. This is especially true if you're stand-ing up against a prevalent idea or popular position. Our kids will find themselves similarly targeted. They must believe that God has equipped them to be able to take that stand. **I will help my children know that God prepares them to stand up for what's right.**

For our struggle is not against flesh and blood, but against the rulers, against the authorities, against the powers of this dark world and against the spiritual forces of evil in the heavenly realms. I wish I could just tell my boys how much God loves them, how much LaFon and I love them, how much their family loves them. I wish I could tell them about how wonderful heaven will be and stop there. I don't really want to get into *the spiritual forces of evil* or the harsh realities of hell. (Frankly, I'm not really clear on how all that works myself.) I'd like to present just the good part and leave out the bad, but I can't because that's not the whole picture. There is a very real struggle between good and evil that plays itself out every day here on earth. The sad truth is, if I never let my child go anywhere or be with anyone other than me, my child would still meet evil face to face, through my sin initially and eventually through his or her own. This is the spiritual conflict that plays out individually and collectively. I have to talk about both parts because I'm made up of both parts, of both flesh and spirit, and so is my child.

This struggle exists not just within me, within my child, and within this world, but also in what Scripture calls *the heavenly realms.* That means there's an entire other dimension where this drama is played out. The drama has two sides — good and evil. So, like it or not, my boys need to understand that both good *and* evil exist. Of course, I'm going to teach them about the goodness of God but I also need to explain as they grow up about evil and what it means. They need to know that evil is powerful in its own right, tricky in presentation and absolutely dedicated to their harm. Gregg and Benjamin also need to know that the struggle they're in, as champions of God, isn't against other people, but rather against the evil that other people *do.* Gregg's already shown a remarkable beginning through his prayer mentioned earlier. After all, I want my kids to emulate Christ in their love for people. I want them to maintain their compassion for others, while at the same time recognizing when people act in unacceptable ways. I want them to come to identify the source of that behavior and to despise it for the destruction it causes. **I will help my children hate evil and love people.**

Therefore put on the full armor of God, so that when the day of evil comes, you may be able to stand your ground, and after you have done everything, to stand. As parents we know that our reaction to things can make a tremendous difference in how our child, in turn, reacts. For example, when one of the boys stubs a toe or scrapes a knee playing, I don't treat the injury like the end of the world. Of course, I make sure I know the extent of the injury and agree with them that it hurts but I don't panic or appear shocked. I'm not shocked because I know that's just part of running or jumping or riding a bike. These types of consequences are *expected.* I want my children to expect the possibility of a cut or scrape as a consequence of learning to play. That way, when the inevitable comes, they are already prepared for it. The stubbed toe or scraped knee does not cause them to retreat inside the house and refuse to go outside.

Dealing with bad things in life is an expected consequence. In a spiritual sense, our children need to know the day of evil will come. This verse doesn't say *if* but *when.* We don't teach them that bad things never happen to good people. We teach them that God knew bad things happening would be a consequence of this life and has carefully constructed a way of protection. We teach them to move from fear of evil to faith in God. Faith in God allows them to stand their ground. God wants Gregg and Benjamin to learn how to stand their ground. I do, too, because I can't be with them every moment. **I will help my children be alert to evil and confident in their ability to stand against it.**

Stand firm then, with the belt of truth buckled around your waist. . . . Now, we're getting into the gear itself. What specifically can we arm our children with, in order to protect them from this evil we know exists, we know they will experience, and need to stand against? The first thing is the truth. Our children need to know the truth. Sounds easy, right? I've got a Bible; I know what the truth is. Surely I can teach my kids the truth! That depends on your understanding of what the word *teach* means.

My children learn from me every day. If it were just a matter of what I say, I might feel better about this. However, my children learn from me through what I say *and* do. They make judgments based upon how I act, what I hold valuable, where I spend my time, how I interact with others. My very life is a schoolroom where my truth is taught and my children are the students. Sometimes, more often than I care to admit, the only truth my children learn is that their father isn't perfect. However, this is still a valuable lesson — because they aren't either.

My life affects their understanding of the truth and understanding truth is vital to their protection. How can I make sure the truth they see in me reflects God's truth? By constantly looking to God myself. I accept the truth that much of how my children view the world, God, and themselves will come from me. When they look at me, therefore, I must reflect Christ. When I don't, I need to confess and ask forgiveness. I want my children to take to heart Hebrews 13:7; I want them to not only imitate me but consider the outcome of my way of life. **I will help my children know God's truth.**

Stand firm then . . . with the breastplate of righteousness in place. A bullet-proof vest, worn by police officers and soldiers, is the closest thing I can think of as the modern-day equivalent of a breastplate. Basically, it's a way to shield your core—the vital organs most vulnerable to a mortal wound. Each of us has a spiritual core that must be protected, and God's armor includes a breastplate of righteousness. If this were made out of my own righteousness, it wouldn't stand up to a single heavy blow! Romans 3:10 very clearly tells me that my righteousness is worthless when it comes to spiritual protection; in fact, it is non-existent. Fortunately, a few more verses down, in verse 21, I'm told where I can get a better breastplate made of sterner stuff: *"This righteousness from God comes through faith in Jesus Christ to all who believe."* The breastplate God is talking about in Ephesians comes from God through faith in Christ.

It's interesting that this breastplate of righteousness is listed after the belt of truth. In order for my child to avoid the mistake of trying to use his or her own breastplate of self-righteousness, he or she needs to understand the truth that there isn't one. Sadly, many children who come from religious families fall into this trap of thinking they're protected by a breastplate of self-righteousness. When the arrows come, they are unprotected and sustain deep injury as a result. In order to prepare my child to be God's champion, I need to avoid a family atmosphere of spiritual superiority that leads to a self-righteous attitude. My children need to understand we are protected by God's righteousness through their faith in Christ. It isn't because LaFon and I are Christians or because they've gone to church their entire lives.

Their righteousness isn't derived out of anything they've done; its source is Christ alone. I want Gregg and Benjamin to understand what really good news that is. Because their righteousness isn't obtained through their own perfection, it can't be lost through their own imperfection. It's safe in Christ. They can mess up — and will — and God still protects them through their faith. **I will help my children find their righteousness in Christ alone.**

Stand firm then... with your feet fitted with the readiness that comes from the gospel of peace. This part of the verse immediately makes me think of Romans 10:15, which says, "How beautiful are the feet of those who bring good news," quoting Isaiah 52:7. I get this vision of my kids happily running to kiss their grandparents or charging into my office at work to give me a hug, but, as I look at this verse, I realize there's something else at play here. This verse doesn't talk about running, it talks about standing firm and being ready.

The more I think about it, the more this verse reminds me of baseball. Seattle is home to the Mariners, a major league baseball team. During the spring and summer months, I love to take the family out to Safeco Field and watch them play. If you've ever seen an opposing team get ready for a batter to hit the ball, they're standing firm and ready. They're up on the balls of their feet, ready to move wherever needed to make the play. I think, in the same way, the gospel allows us to be ready. This isn't a heavy-footed, slow-moving type of readiness. Rather, I see this as a springy, nimble, sure-footedness that allows us to move and respond through the word. After all, 1 Peter 3:15 tells us to "always be prepared to give an answer to everyone who asks you to give a reason for the hope that you have." This is how I want my children to be — standing firm in their faith yet agile enough to give that answer, to respond to that situation. **I will help my children be spiritually agile and ready.**

In addition to this, take up the shield of faith, with which you can extinguish all the flaming arrows of the evil one. This is a profound truth; this verse says that faith is sufficient to defeat the plans of the evil one. Faith is powerful. So, what is faith? Hebrews 11:1 says, "Now faith is being sure of what we hope for and certain of what we do not see." Faith doesn't just extinguish some or most of the flaming arrows coming at us, it handles them all. If my children must enter into a spiritual battlefield, I want them to have a shield of faith. So, how do I help cultivate faith in my children? By teaching them to have hope in God and, more, to trust that hope. If they have no hope, they can have no faith. Just as my children learn truth from me, they also learn hope from me. What do I hope for them? Do I live my life with hope? Do I rely only upon what is visible or do I trust in the future and place my hope in God? Is my hope for my children based solely upon who they are now, at this moment, or is it based on trust in what God can and will do in each of their lives? **I will help my children learn faith by having faith in them.**

Take the helmet of salvation. . . . Have you ever watched a movie of medieval jousting or sword play, where the knight carefully dons each fitted piece of armor? Have you ever seen one forget the helmet? Of course not! A helmet protects your head. If your head isn't protected, it doesn't make much sense to go to the trouble of protecting the rest of your body. One hard knock to the head and you're done. God, therefore, gives His armor the ultimate helmet, one made of His salvation.

This is a helmet that's tailored to the shape of our need, fitting it perfectly. God tailors salvation to each of us, filling in our individual weaknesses and needs, remaking us into the image of Christ. Your child has a helmet of salvation specially fitted by God. This salvation provides your child with the ultimate in spiritual protection. That is, of course, if you put it on.

Some people don't believe that God will save them. Oh, they believe He is capable of saving them but fear, when it comes right down to it, that He won't. Guilt and shame cause them to leave their helmet behind when entering a spiritual battle. They don't put it on because they don't believe it was meant for them. Is it any wonder they are defeated? The helmet of salvation is provided, but each of us must take it up and put it on. Make sure your child not only knows that God can save him or her but also that He *will*. **I will help my children believe in their own personal salvation.**

Take . . . the sword of the Spirit, which is the word of God. This book is a tool but it is not a sword. There is no substitute for the Word of God. Your child needs to fall in love with God's Word. In the heat of battle, what other people say about God's Word is not nearly as effective as God's Word itself. God puts himself at the point of battle by making himself the Sword. We know from John 1:1, speaking of Christ, that "in the beginning was the Word, and the Word was with God, and the Word was God." Christ himself acts as our weapon, protecting us and defending us. This sword of God is also able to enlighten us to the true nature of the enemy's schemes and attacks. Hebrews 4:12 says "For the word of God is living and active. Sharper than any double-edged sword, it penetrates even to dividing soul and spirit, joints and marrow; it judges the thoughts and attitudes of the heart." In spiritual warfare today, often the attacks are not frontal attacks; rather, they are backdoor, sideways, and end runs around our faith, attitudes, and actions. We need a weapon at our disposal that is able to see through the deception and expose the truth.

Like any weapon, our children need to know how to use it properly. With the Word of God, the way to use it properly is to know it, embrace it, embody it. The Word is not meant to bolster what we think; the Word is meant to reveal what God thinks. This is when a weapon truly becomes effective; when it becomes an extension of who you are. With God's spiritual weapon, its effectiveness is shown when we become an extension of the Word. This is the level of spiritual integration I hope for my children. This love of the Word needs to start young and be nurtured throughout childhood.

Your children will love what you love. They will value what you value. If the Bible is a book that's collecting dust on your coffee table, it's an unused sword. **I will help my children love and respect God's Word.**

And pray in the Spirit on all occasions with all kinds of prayers and requests. I've heard and read other presentations of the armor of God and several have ended at the previous verse. After all, the next two don't make any mention of armor. To me, though, they are meant just as much for God's champion. This verse reminds God's champion that he or she is never alone in battle. The Spirit is there, instantly available, through every kind of struggle. Armies are made and battles are won by superior lines of communication. In this spiritual struggle, our lines of communication to God are always open. He doesn't censor our prayers but extends an invitation to pray *on all occasions, with all kinds of prayers and requests.* He is the commander and the quartermaster, leading the battle and providing the materials and reinforcements needed to win that battle. My child isn't a Lone Ranger but a fully supplied champion of God. **I will help my children to pray in all situations.**

With this in mind, be alert and always keep on praying for all the saints. The struggle is more than just any one battle. God's champion needs to recognize that he or she is joined by a great multitude of fellow soldiers. Paul even uses this term when speaking of other Christians in his letters to the church in Philippi and to his Christian brother, Philemon. This is an important metaphor and visualization. I need to know that there are others fighting along-side me. It restores my faith and keeps me going. When I lag and fall behind, there are others to pick me up and carry me until I'm able to stand on my own again.

Children need to see themselves within the context of spiritual family. You do this first by being supportive of the spiritual goals and efforts of the immediate family. When your child falters spiritually, you're there to help him or her up. When you falter, you allow your child to be there for you. Immediate and spiritual families strengthen bonds by praying for and with each other.

There's a bigger world, a broader faith-community out there than just your family or your congregation. In our home, we have one of those talking globes. When you use a special pen and touch a place on the globe, you hear a recording tell you about location, size, population, and facts about that particular place. We use this to show the boys about special places in the world where Christians need prayers. We pray for missionaries from our church and in our own family, like my sister and her family who serve on the mission field. By praying for saints all around the world, your child can feel a part of the global cause for Christ. He or she can begin to realize how big this world is and how big God is. Remember, there's no guarantee that your child, God's champion, was meant to stay in your city, state, or even country. Regardless of where your champion lives, he or she can participate everywhere by becoming aware of and praying for saints around the world. **I will help my children be aware of God at work in the world.**

Training Ground

Parents Promise

By looking at the armor of God, we've seen the protection God has prepared for your champion. I want to take a moment here and reinforce the one sentence affirmations at the end of each verse or phrase discussion. These are how I condensed what I heard the Scripture say to me. If they resonate with you, that's great. If not, I encourage you to read over the Ephesians passage and come up with some definitive statements to help you focus on how to prepare your child to don his or her armor as God's champion. Each piece of God's armor is a spiritual truth that you can teach and your child can integrate into understanding the world, God, and self.

Whether you use these or your own, I encourage you to incorporate them when praying for and teaching your child. There's nothing wrong in letting your child know how you are praying for him or her. Copy these commitment statements down and post them in a visible place. Use them during family devotionals or at prayer time with your child. Allow your child to know your heart where his or her spiritual life is concerned.

> I will help my child know that a mighty God is his/her source of strength.
>
> I will help my child know that God prepares him/her to stand up for what's right.
>
> I will help my child hate evil and love people.
>
> I will help my child be alert to evil and confident in his/her ability to stand against it.
>
> I will help my child know God's truth.
>
> I will help my child find his/her righteousness in Christ alone.
>
> I will help my child be spiritually agile and ready.
>
> I will help my child learn faith by having faith in him/her.
>
> I will help my child believe in his/her own personal salvation.
>
> I will help my child love and respect God's Word.
>
> I will help my child learn to pray in all situations.
>
> I will help my child be aware of God at work in the world.

Champion's Creed

Now that you've come up with your Parent's Promise, I want you to work with your child to create a Champion's Creed. These are affirmation statements that your child can learn and even memorize that capture significant truths from God's Word. Children need to know who they are, accept who they are, and be confident in who they are. Using Scripture, create a Champion's Creed for each of your children.

Here is one that's used at the Christian school where my children attend. This is actually recited from memory each morning by the class of kindergarteners! I was so impressed with this "renewing of the mind," I asked the principal, Jim Davis, if I could use it in this book. He gave his permission and I share it with you, as an example of what you can do to help your child create his or her own Champion's Creed:

This is the day that the Lord hath made. I will rejoice and be glad in it.

Today I will grow as Jesus grew becoming strong in my spirit, mind, and body.

God is working in me to act according to His purpose.

I am a child of God because Jesus is my Lord.

I am made in His image.

God's love has been placed in my heart.

Everywhere I go I plant seeds of love.

People are blessed by my life.

I am bold, strong, and very courageous.

I will do great works.

I fear not for God is with me.

I am thankful to God I live in America and will always speak well of it.

Since Jesus is my Lord, my time in school will be good.

I have the mind of Christ.

I can learn all things.

I can do all things.

I never give up.

I never quit.

I never fail.

I was born to win.

I love the Lord my God with all my heart, all my soul, and all my mind.

I'm still amazed by seeing those five and six year olds reciting this creed from memory. They were enthusiastic and happy to affirm these things about themselves. You could see the energy and encouragement it gave them. You could hear it, too! I'm sure Jim wouldn't mind if this became your child's creed, so use it if you will. Depending upon your child and your situation, feel free to come up with one of your own. Whichever, encourage your child to memorize their Champion's Creed. These are simple, age-appropriate statements, based in Scripture, that your child can have readily available through memory, when needed.

So much of what a child thinks about him or herself comes from the verbal and non-verbal messages received each day from other people and situations. Not all of these messages will be positive; in fact, many of them are negative. This is part of the spiritual warfare waging around your child. Being able to call up the most positive truth of God is a bulwark against this onslaught. A memorized truth is an accessible truth.

As your child grows, this Champion's Creed can be updated, revised, rewritten. Perhaps you can use the occasion of your child's birthday to re-write the Creed each year and then incorporate it as a focal point of your personal prayers for your child that year.

Father, I thank You for the protection You've provided to my child. I confess I'm fearful of the battlefields to come, so please help me to trust You. Allow my faith in Your protection to teach my child to have faith in You, too.

Section 2

Finding
Their Fruit

Helping our kids discover their gifts is like an Easter egg hunt. Some eggs are more obvious, right on top of the surface of your child, and some are hidden, requiring more persistence and ingenuity to find them. Just because you don't see the eggs right away, doesn't mean they're not there; you just have to look harder and smarter.

I sometimes think God is like that with gifts. Some, we know about right away. They're on the very surface of our being and pretty obvious. You walk up and there it is, sitting on top of the grass. Others, though, require deeper searching and more thought — hidden in the crook of a tree or the hollow of a rock. Go ahead and admit it — these are much more fun!

It's perfectly all right for our kids to do some searching to find all the gifts God has hidden inside them. The more they learn about God and understand about His nature and character, the easier it will be for them to figure out where those gifts might be hidden. In finding their own gifts, they find out about God.

The gifts of our children are not always immediately visible or known. Sometimes they require a journey of discovery to identify their gifts. It can be difficult to remember it's not a question of whether they have gifts but what those gifts are. When we fail to see our children as gifted, it is not a lack of giftedness on their part, it's a lack of vision on our part. Every child is a gifted child; this is God's promise.

> *And God is able to make all grace abound to you, so that in all things at all times, having all that you need, you will abound in every good work* (2 Cor. 9:8).

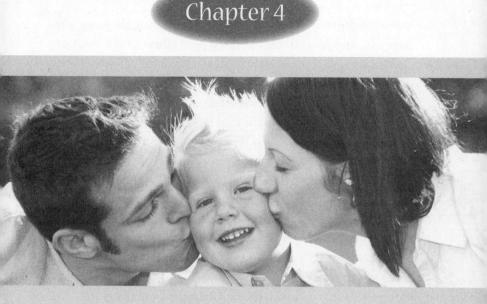

Chapter 4

Cultivating
Universal Gifts

Now to him who is able to do immeasurably more than all we ask or imagine, according to his power that is at work within us (Eph. 3:20).

I want my children to succeed. Okay, I admit it; I want them to do more than that — I want them to excel. I guess I want it to be perfectly clear to the world how extraordinary and amazing my children are! So my ambitions for them as a parent are pretty big. I want to support them and give them what they need to hit life running. Are my hopes and dreams for my kids big? Sure!

It's good to know, I'm not alone in this. God is as pleased and proud and ambitious for my children as I am, even more so. He has BIG plans for them. In fact, Paul tells us in the Corinthian passage at the start of this section that God's plans are pretty all-encompassing; they include *every good work*. That's a tall order, but God is willing to give whatever it takes to equip my children. He is willing to give *all grace in all things at all times for all need*. If I ever doubt His willingness to provide such largesse, I need only look to the One He's already given. God has a proven track record of providing for us in a BIG way.

I can understand this in global terms, in thinking of the Church as a whole. I can see how God has BIG plans for the Church at large. It's a little harder to see when it comes down to my small family unit. Do I really believe that God is sufficient for *every need* of my child? I must tell myself over and over again, "Yes!" In this, I echo the statement of the father in Mark 9:25 who cried out to Jesus, "I do believe; help me overcome my unbelief!" I do believe God is able; I just need help with my unbelief when it comes to my kids.

One way I've found to fortify faith where my kids are concerned is through visualization. It helps me to visualize my children armored and protected — like in Ephesians — when they leave my front door. It's comforting to see them as defended by Scripture and guarded by the righteousness of Christ when out of my sight. For those times when it's hard for me to see what God has in mind for my boys, it helps to visualize them as a work of God, under construction. If it's hard for you to visualize the final product God has in mind for your child, I invite you to see your son or daughter as a God-directed work-in-progress. Visualize the positive future God has in mind for your child.

First Corinthians 6:19 says your child's destiny is as a temple of the Holy Spirit. (Depending upon the age of your child, he or she may simply seem like a holy *terror* now, but again, God has plans.) Temples aren't built overnight. Nor are they built in a haphazard way. Even the tabernacle, the portable temple for the Children of Israel wandering in the desert, was laid out in Scripture with precise instructions. From chapter 25 through the end of the book at chapter 40, Exodus is full of the minute, exact details God reveals as the chosen design for His "sacred residence" (Exod. 25:8). That's how

I need to think of my children. In a way, Gregg and Benjamin are "sacred residences," little tabernacles — pint-sized portable temples of the Living God.

I'm not very handy with *things*. Some people have a fix-it gene; I don't. My gift is more around fixing people. I have a psychological toolbox, not a literal one. That's why I love my friend Dave. Dave was born with a hammer in his hand. He's a handy guy and can build or fix just about anything. With a growing business of multiple branches, and two boys at home, I seem to need Dave a lot.

If I break out in a cold sweat over a minor building project around my home or office, you can imagine how daunting it is to think about "building" a little tabernacle in my child. How am I supposed to know what sort of foundation and structure to give Gregg as he's growing up, in order to prepare him for the tasks ahead? Benjamin is in preschool! How am I supposed to know what God has in mind for him years down the road?

When I'm faced with an earthly building dilemma, I look to Dave. When I'm faced with a spiritual building dilemma, I look to God. While I may not know the specific tasks God has in mind for my children — or the outside of their tabernacles, if you will — God has told me the sort of foundation He wants for all of His children. Gregg and Benjamin are temples of the Holy Spirit and their spiritual foundations are called the fruit of the Spirit, found in Galatians 5:22–23: *"But the fruit of the Spirit is love, joy, peace, patience, kindness, goodness, faithfulness, gentleness and self-control. Against such things, there is no law."*

Fruitful Foundations

Unlike specific spiritual gifts given to individuals by God to accomplish a specific purpose, the fruits of the Spirit are meant for all. We can be confident, then, that we're in complete agreement with God when we teach and model these spiritual characteristics. For what champion would not benefit from a solid grounding in love, joy, peace, patience, kindness, goodness, faithfulness, gentleness, and self-control? From this foundation comes the framework for every other gift. Many of these gifts may take years to be manifested, but the fruit of the Spirit can be worked on right now, no matter the age of your child.

Don't be deceived; temples take hard work (reference the Old Testament Book of Ezra if you have questions). Even when God provided the instructions, the scope and sequence of work and, in many cases, even the building materials, people still had to do the construction. Was God with the people, guiding and sustaining them in their work? Yes, but they still had to labor to get the job done.

Birthing a child is called labor. Building a tabernacle or a champion is also laborious. You've got to roll up your sleeves and get your hands dirty. You need to prioritize your life and channel effort and energy into the building of your children. These attributes are gifts from God through the Spirit but they must be developed and internalized. Two year olds are not naturally patient. Seven year olds are not automatically kind. Gentleness is not guaranteed in a 9 year old. Thirteen year olds don't always exhibit self-control. Faith can be an issue for a 16 year old.

So, how do you build on this foundation God intends for your child? You know these are provided by Him, but you also realize they must be bolstered by you. No matter the age of your child, there are a few simple steps you can take as a parent to help your child cultivate these spiritual fruits.

Make fruit a part of your day. Teaching children is often done most effectively by modeling. We've already talked about how important it is for you to emulate the spiritual characteristics you want to develop in your children. You teach love by being loving. You model joy by expressing it yourself. By valuing peace, you pass on its value to your children. When patience is called for, you show it and your children will learn. It isn't about what you say alone, it's about how your actions line up with your words. If they are out of whack, your child's foundations will be wobbly and unsteady.

These aren't unrealistic expectations, either. It's not like an architect expecting her child to grow up to design buildings, or a physician planning medical school for his five year old. These aren't individualized gifts, given only to a chosen few. They are available to everyone and expected of those who love God and call on the name of Christ. They aren't optional; they're required. They are required for life and for the arenas God has planned for your champion.

Again, the time to teach these attributes to your children are when they are most called for in yourself. My kids are sharp. They have a razor-sharp sense of fairness and equity (what kid doesn't!). Constantly, they sift through what I do and match it up to what I say. In doing this, they evaluate both. Because of this, I want the concepts of love, joy, peace, patience, kindness, goodness, faithfulness, gentleness, and self-control to be a core subject, not a special elective. I want my kids to be surrounded by these lessons on a daily, ongoing basis. This is natural evangelism, at the home level. Deuteronomy 11:19 puts it this way, "Teach them to your children, talking about them when you sit at home and when you walk along the road, when you lie down and when you get up." Serve up hearty helpings of spiritual fruit each day to build up the foundations of your champion. If our bodies need five-plus servings of fruit a day to be healthy, imagine what our souls need. Help your child make each day a nine-plus day!

Know when the fruit is ripe. I so much look forward to the men my boys are becoming, it's hard for me to remember sometimes they are just children. I want them to learn patience *now!* Of course, putting it that way just illustrates how foolish it is. Fruit takes time to ripen. In fact, if you try to harvest it too early, it's stunted and hard and bitter. If I expect too much too soon from my children, they will be the same emotionally — stunted, hard, and bitter. For this reason, I take to heart God's admonition in Ephesians 6:4, "Fathers, do not exasperate your children; instead, bring them up in the training and instruction of the Lord." I am reminded, again, that this is a process.

My job isn't to harvest the fruit but to do all I can to help it ripen at the right time. God is in charge of the harvest. First Corinthians 3:7–9 says, "So neither he who plants or he who waters is anything, but only God, who makes things grow. The man who plants and the man who waters have one purpose, and each will be rewarded according to his own labor. For we are God's fellow-workers; you are God's field, God's building." Speaking about our kids, you could paraphrase the verses this way: *So neither the parent who plants nor the parent who waters is anything, but only God, who makes your child grow. The parent who plants and the parent who waters have one purpose, and each will be rewarded for what they impart to their child. For parents are in this together with God; the child is God's field, God's building.*

Teach your child to recognize fruit. Teach your children the fruit of the Spirit. Talk about the qualities of love, joy, peace, patience, kindness, goodness, faithfulness, gentleness, and self-control. Instruct your child in the differences between them and how they are manifested in the daily life situations that arise. Love isn't doing what the other person wants all the time. Joy isn't happiness. Peace isn't capitulation. Patience isn't putting up with evil. Kindness isn't avoiding conflict. Goodness isn't determined only by what a person does. Faithfulness isn't blindly following. Gentleness isn't soft. Self-control isn't self-righteous. Each fruit has its unique shape, flavor, and nutrition for the soul. Allow your child to taste and savor each one. In this way, your child will not only be blessed but will be learning how to be a blessing to others.

Fruit of the Month Club

My children are entering into their school experience. As I'm an older father (in my forties), this has proved enlightening. It's been a while since I was in school myself. One thing I've noticed is how schools are integrating character development into curriculum. LaFon and I have chosen to put our boys in a local Christian school where biblical characteristics are taught, but I've also become aware of this type of teaching in the secular realm, as well. I shouldn't be surprised, I guess, but even secular schools have discovered the need for children to learn positive attributes such as compassion, kindness, patience, perseverance, trustworthiness, and respect. Many of the schools in the district where we live take a component of character and stress it for the month. They call it a variety of names but it's really Fruit of the Month, to me. God's wisdom is woven throughout this world, even when it's not identified as such. I wish all children could know the basis for these attributes but I'm still glad they're being taught.

These attributes aren't just taught for one month and then forgotten about. Rather, each attribute builds upon the others. This emphasis goes on year after year. Attribute by attribute. Year after year. Step by step. This is the way we all learn; it says so in Psalm 37:23: "If the LORD delights in a man's way, he makes his steps firm." He doesn't say he makes his leaps firm, but his steps. Day by day, month by month, year by year, fruit by fruit.

Fruit Friendly

Whether my children are in a Christian school, a secular school, an organized sports team, a neighborhood club, or activity, I need to make sure that the environment is fruit-friendly. How will my children learn the value of gentleness if they're on a team where the coach wants to win at any cost? How can they learn joy if they're in a classroom with a hyper-critical teacher? As much as I'm able, I need to be aware of the nutrients — the actions, attitudes, and attributes of others — my children are exposed to.

This means I need to be aware of the other influences on their lives and their development. Just as the owner of a creek needs to be aware of what the neighbor is doing upstream, I need to know what's trickling its way into the heart and mind of my child. I should know which way the wind is blowing if there's a nearby source of pollution and make sure my child is protected. I need to know if we're due for some freezing weather, so I can protect the seedlings growing in my child. It isn't possible to predict every negative influence, but I can sure take steps to mitigate the ones I know about.

The Breakfast of Champions

Fruit is great for breakfast. Frankly, it's great all day long. This fruit of the Spirit is the food to nourish the soul of my child — God's champion. What I love about this fruit is it's for everyone. My child doesn't need to have some sort of special destiny or display special talents in order to enjoy this fruit. They are universal. I

may not know what the future holds for my little champion, but
I can know that love, joy, peace, patience, kindness, goodness,
faithfulness, gentleness, and self-control will be part of it. I can
know that these attributes are *integral* to that future, its basis and
foundation.

God has chosen these gifts for my child. It is His will that my
child grow in each of them. I must remember that I'm not the only
one working on instilling these characteristics. God is actively engaged in their spiritual education. Like the previous passage says,
God's in charge of the field, of the building.

I must expect, then, that God is going to provide my child with
learning opportunities. There will be times when my child is called
upon to act in a loving way, to show patience or practice self-control.
When these times come, I need to step back and allow God to work
with my child. It's not my job to rush in, to save the day. My job is
to watch and allow my child to choose to use the gifts he or she has
been given. Sometimes he will and sometimes he won't. Whichever,
it's a learning opportunity and a chance to examine the fruit to see
if it's ripe. It's a chance for my child to learn that God — not me
— is the source of their strength.

Each day is a training ground for your child. Each day will
have opportunities to grow and strengthen these gifts of God. At
times, these opportunities will come when you're with your child.
Other times, they will come when your child is being cared for or
taught by another person. It's important, therefore, to know about
the significant events in your child's day. Inquire of the adults your
child has been with. Also ask your child. Spend some time talking
about what happened during the day. Gauge reactions and listen
carefully to the words used. Observe your child's demeanor. Be
alert to how you can use the events of the day to reinforce spiritual
attributes.

This should not be a modern equivalent of the Inquisition.
Remember, God says to do this naturally, as you sit together or walk
down the road. You can do it watching a video or playing catch in
the park. You can do it cooking dinner or going over homework.

It's not just you lecturing your child about what to do. Give your child a chance to explain situations and tell you what he or she thought about it. How did he feel? What did she say? Allow your child to come up with the "right" answers. This is part of their discovery. As these attributes are acknowledged and appreciated by your child, they become more and more a part of who they are. You are working toward the day when these characteristics spring forth from your child instead of being superimposed on your child by you.

Training Ground

We've talked a lot about the fruit of the Spirit. Close your eyes (or, at least, don't go back and look) and recite them from memory. There are nine of them. (Come on, if you can remember all seven dwarves, surely you can remember nine fruit!). Let's see, they are love, joy, peace, patience, kindness, gentleness, faithfulness, and self-control. Nope, that's eight — missed one. Okay, go back and look! Goodness — I missed goodness!

Even after reading them over (even after writing about them), it's still hard to remember them all. For that reason, I want you to memorize them. In this way, you can be alert to them as they relate to your child. Next, I'd like you to get a piece of paper and write each characteristic down, with space between. Over the next week, look for examples of each of these attributes being played out in the life of your child. Was there a special instance where your child was able to be loving to someone else? What about goodness (the one I forgot), did your child do or say something that was just out of the goodness of his or her heart? Was your child faithful this week in some way?

Keeping track of these in an intentional way will accomplish a couple of good things. For one, it will encourage you to take time with your child each day and really talk about your child's day. Not you talking *at* your child but talking *with* your child. Secondly, you'll be focusing on examples of good things happening in your child's life. If you and your child are going through a difficult time, this can motivate you to keep working through it. (If you haven't gone through one of these periods with your child, remember this, because you will.)

Begin to see your child as already having these characteristics. This tracking isn't so you can find them, but rather so you can learn to recognize them. These gifts are promised by God. He hasn't bypassed your child. They may be covered up by a three-year-old tantrum or a seven-year-old pout, but they're still there! Repeat to yourself: God is able to give my child the ability to love, to know joy, to value peace, to practice patience, to show kindness, to be good, to exhibit faithfulness, and to model gentleness and self-control.

God, as I read over these characteristics You've ordained for my child, I realize how much I need them myself! May we both grow in them, as we grow closer to each other and to You. I thank You for this little champion, this little tabernacle, You've entrusted to my care. Help me to value and appreciate these promised gifts in my child, to never take them for granted, and to always cherish and nurture them.

Chapter 5

Uncovering Personal Gifts

It was he who gave some to be apostles, some to be prophets, some to be evangelists, and some to be pastors and teachers, to prepare God's people for works of service, so that the body of Christ may be built up until we all reach unity in the faith and in the knowledge of the Son of God and become mature, attaining to the whole measure of the fullness of Christ (Eph. 4:11–13).

Just as each of us has one body with many members, and these members do not all have the same function, so in Christ we who are many form one body, and each member belongs to all the others (Rom. 12:4–5).

There are different kinds of gifts, but the same Spirit.
There are different kinds of service, but the same Lord. There
are different kinds of working, but the same God works all of
them in all men. . . . As it is, there are many parts, but one
body (1 Cor. 12:4–20).

It is a profound mystery that God is transforming us into one Body — Christ — while allowing us to retain our unique individuality. Further, He uses that individuality to create the many parts of the one Body He intends. This means I don't need to give up who I am in Christ; neither does my child. All the quirky traits and the idiosyncrasies don't need to be drummed out of my child in order for him or her to fulfill God's destiny. It may be that those very same quirks and idiosyncrasies are foreshadowing the part of the Body God intends for your child to be.

Each child, we know from Psalm 139, is formed by God and comes into this world with a full-blown personality. At the beginning of this book, I told you about how different Gregg and Benjamin are from each other. I'm nothing like my sister. LaFon is different from her brother and sister. Same family, different individuals. It isn't just a by-product of nature, it is the specific design of God. It is through this incredible diversity that His power is shown through our unity in Christ.

We are called to be like Christ and exhibit His characteristics. God encourages us by giving His Spirit, who in turn gives us the very attributes of Christ. That's what we talked about in the last chapter. In this way, we merge and become one in Christ. This is our collective destiny. Gregg and Benjamin, LaFon and I are destined to become one in Christ.

God has an individual destiny mapped out for each one of us. He alone has the capacity to comprehend and direct such a complex weaving together of lives and personalities, talents and gifts. Each of us is an individual thread woven together to form a single cloth. Your child has a thread of his or her own. It is not like every other thread. Rather, God has purposely made it different in order to complete His tapestry of diversity. There are no cookie-cutter Christians.

That gives me great comfort when I look at my boys. Because they are so different and react to the world is such diverse ways, it would be difficult to think that, for example, serious, empirical Gregg was more what God had in mind than impulsive, emotional Benjamin. Or that spontaneous, energetic Benjamin is more useful to God than methodical, complex Gregg. No, Gregg and Benjamin are perfect, just the way they are. They don't have to be like each other; they don't have to be like me or LaFon. They can simply be who they are and allow God to continue what He started by positioning them as the perfect part in His perfect whole.

They do not need to look the same to be used the same. When a body is walking, both arms and legs are moving. They are not the same but they are used the same. In fact, the motion of the arms counterbalances the movement of the legs and allows for balance. In the same way, children can be completely different from each other but still similarly useful to God. It's important for your child to know this, so he or she won't be discouraged if they don't look just like someone else. It's important for you to know this, in order to avoid partiality or favoritism between children. It's important for extended family to know this to avoid similar value judgments. If you want to have a favorite flavor of ice cream, go ahead. But don't extend that preference to deciding between children.

Picking Out the Part

Even though my children are young, I can already see personality traits and characteristics unique to each. Gregg is tenacious and focused. Benjamin is intuitive and responsive. As each of them grows, these tendencies will mature and solidify, but I doubt they will ever completely go away. We are who we are; we are who God made us to be. My empathy for people is as inborn in me as my eye color. If you ask my mom, she'll tell you I was always this way. I doubt she thought I'd be the head of a mental health and chemical dependency agency when I grew up but I also doubt it surprises her much that I am.

Who I am and how God made me fits His plan. He has use in
the Body for someone like me. He has use in the Body for someone
like Gregg, and like Benjamin. I don't really understand, at this point,
how all of that will work out but I am confident it will. It's not really
my job as a parent to try to figure that out. I have faith in the plan,
in the purpose God has for my child. When I start putting my child
in a box, saying, "Surely God will use him this way or, certainly
God could never use her that way," I'm putting myself in charge of
my child's destiny. I've just yanked the wheel back from God and
demanded to be in the driver's seat of my child's life. Frankly, I'm
not that good of a spiritual driver. I need to allow God to direct how
Gregg and Benajmin will fit into His plan.

Now it may be apparent early on what sort of unique gifts and
talents one or both of my boys will have. I've known parents whose
children showed characteristics or aptitudes almost from infancy.
Their lives followed an almost predictable pattern, leading them
to a certain profession or vocation. I don't believe, however, that's
the case for most of us as parents. I just don't think many of us can
really know what direction our children's lives will take. We don't
have a clue what they will *do*. We can have a clue who they will *be*.
Childhood and adolescence are meant to mold and shape personality
and character. Ultimately, this is what is the measure of a person,
not necessarily what they do.

Too many of us equate gifts and talents with skills or aptitudes
and, in a way, I guess they are. Certainly there are musicians, for
example, who show extraordinary talent early. It's obvious to all that
their talent isn't born out of practice but is an innate gift, honed
and perfected by practice. There are children who are athletic and
naturally gifted in sports. Tiger Woods, for example, could swing a
golf club properly at an early age. We call these people gifted.

Now, it is possible for people gifted in this way to be champions
for God. One such individual who comes to mind is the great NFL
running back Shaun Alexander. An incredible athlete on the football
field, Shaun is no less an incredible champion for God, through
the witness of his life and the testimony of his lips. Would Shaun

be a champion for God if he wasn't a football player? I certainly hope so, because the tenure of a professional sports star is a short one. I want Shaun to excel on God's field a lot longer than he'll be on a football field!

Sometimes I'm concerned that as parents we believe our children's destiny as God's champion is tied up in what our child does. I think the truth of it is that God's champions are proven through who they are. The fields of battle will change as will our child as he or she grows and matures. What they do will change. Remember, current studies show that the average American will change jobs and careers numerous times over the course of their lives. We should not confuse the part we play at work with the part we play in the body of Christ.

As the parent of a champion, then, I need to keep my eyes focused on the true prize. The true prize is not entrance into an Ivy League school or a professional sports team. The true prize is found in the content of my child's character, in the immortal words of Dr. Martin Luther King Jr. While I need to be alert and support my children's choices for what they do, I need to be even more alert and supportive of the special ways God has gifted who they are.

Let's take a look at some of the ways God tells us He gifts His people, in order for all of us to become mature in Christ. Ephesians 4 tells us that God gifts people to be apostles, prophets, evangelists, preachers, and teachers. Romans 12 says there are gifts of, again, prophesy and teaching, but also serving, encouraging, contributing, in leadership, and in showing mercy. These are all special gifts of the Spirit, given to individuals in order to build up the Body, the Church.

As you become more and more familiar with your child, I urge you to take as much time, energy, and care in cultivating these gifts as you do those that tend to gain more "worldly" attention. A child who shows mercy, for example, should be valued as highly as a child of high intellect. A child whose gift is compassion may grow up to work in the mission field in a foreign country, never known as a highly lucrative profession. A child whose gift is encouragement may spend a great deal of his or her time and energy devoted to the "success" of others without necessarily producing anything in this life to show for it. A child who is blessed by God to be a servant often languishes out of the spotlight of this world. In all of these things, be aware that "God chose the foolish things of the world to shame the wise; God chose the weak things of the world to shame the strong" (1 Cor. 1:27). Do not look for only those gifts the world values in your children. If you do, you'll fail to really see the glory of God that is your child.

We look at the differences in people and use them to create a hierarchy of value. This hierarchy of value does not lead to unity but ultimately to division. This division leads to jealousy, envy, hatred, bitterness, and misunderstanding. God's remarkable personal gifts are given to bring all of us closer together and closer to the Lord. Don't predetermine what gifts you will find acceptable in your child. Don't predetermine which gifts mean God's favor in your child. Don't predetermine the spiritual value of your child by the gifts God has chosen for him or her.

Different in Gifts — Alike in Love

I am struck, when reading through the passages at the beginning of this chapter, how many times these statements about gifts are juxtaposed next to admonitions to love one another. The last two passages, from 1 Corinthians 12, begin a discussion that culminates in that beautiful treatise on love in 1 Corinthians 13. Before we're told what love is, we're told all of our special gifts are nothing if we don't have it. The sad truth is that our differences sometimes hinder our ability to love one another. We begin to make value judgments on the gift, thinking that God loves one person more because of the gift he or she has been given. What a devastation it is for a parent to think God values one child over another, because of the gifts evident in each child.

In an earlier chapter, I spoke about the difficulty partiality has within a family. We saw biblical examples of how favoritism and partiality lead to animosity and even murderous intent. By the time Paul writes his first letter to the Corinthians, it doesn't appear much has changed. He even has to admonish Christians not to start assigning human value to divine gifts. The highest gift he says is love, something God is and gives to everyone. Let me repeat that — the greatest, highest, best gift anyone will ever receive from God is not reserved for a chosen few; it is freely given by God to everyone through His Son — freely given by God and to be freely given by us.

Does this mean you shouldn't watch for special gifts God has placed in your children? Absolutely not! As the parent, you'll need to be alert and aware so you can support and encourage. Just don't be confused that the part in the Body God has designed your child for will automatically be manifested in the career or job your child does.

So, what do you do as a parent, then, to encourage and support the spiritual gifts God has given to your children? Get to know your children. Find out what they are interested in. Be alert to unusual maturity they exhibit in a particular characteristic or attribute. Is your child especially empathetic? Does he have a heart for suffering in the world? Does she show an ability to persuade others to do what's right? Is he a generous soul, giving of his own means to help others? Does she always seek to build up others in the family? You could be seeing the first signs of the extraordinary gifts God has given your child, which become more apparent as he or she grows and matures.

In addition, watch for special situations or circumstances where it seems a certain trait or tendency is being challenged. It may be that God is already working at that gift, stretching it to become even bigger. That is why I caution you not to automatically jump in to rescue your child in a difficult situation. This could be God at work, exercising His budding champion.

You simply may not know, until after your child leaves the house, how God is going to use him or her to further His kingdom. That isn't part of the fine print on the parenting document. In the absence of clear direction, then, do everything you can to promote the good qualities you see in your child. Think outside the box when it comes to how your child may be gifted. Think outside the box in how your child can demonstrate his or her gift, in various situations in life.

Again, here are some particular spiritual gifts the Bible mentions:

- The gift of prophecy — one who understands divine inspiration and declares the purposes of God.

- The gift of evangelism or preaching — one who is the bringer of good tidings.

- The gift of teaching — one who can not only know a thing but explain a thing.

- The gift of serving — one who is able to grasp the heart of Jesus.

- The gift of encouraging — one who brings comfort and refreshment.

- The gift of healing — one who knows how to bring relief and health.

- The gift of contributing — one who has the means and the will to give to others.

- The gift of leadership — one who accepts the point position for God.

- The gift of mercy — one who demonstrates the ability to forego justice.

Training Ground

Think about your children. Even if they are small, evaluate the characteristics and propensities they already are showing. Think about what these may mean for your child as he or she grows. Meditate on your child. Pray for your child and ask God to reveal to you the areas He wants you to strengthen and encourage in your child. Thank God for the way He made your child. Give Him the glory and pray for His protection and guidance as you raise your child.

God, I thank You for my child. Help me to see the gifts You have placed inside. Prevent me from harming or hindering those gifts. Give me confidence in those gifts. I thank You that You have not left it up to me to determine what those gifts should be. I confess I could not provide for my child as completely as You. Help me to be humble and accept the gifts You have placed in my child. Guard me from jealousy or disappointment. I want to place Your value on these gifts, not the world's. Help me to see my child's giftedness through Your eyes.

Molding the Whole Champion

Your child exists as an emotional, physical, intellectual, and spiritual being. All of these aspects will contribute to the expression of their God-given gifts. Like seeds, these gifts are planted within the very core of your child. In order for them to fully flower, the whole person must be cultivated. Just as a flower has roots, a stem, leaves, and petals, your child has different aspects of his or her life that — though different — all work together for the good of your child. When all aspects are respected and cared for, the whole child, like the whole flower, can blossom, grow, and give joy and color to this world.

> *Love the Lord your God with all your heart and with all your soul and with all your mind and with all your strength* (Mark 12:30).

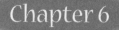

Chapter 6

Whole
Hearted

Search me, O God, and know my heart (Ps. 139:23).

The passage that started this section says that we are to love the Lord with all our heart, soul, mind, and strength. I like to view this verse as saying we are to love and honor God with our heart — emotions, our soul — spirit, our mind — intellect, and our strength — physical bodies. This is molding the whole champion. In the midst of this spiritual battle, our children need comprehensive, whole-person development. The enemy is looking for any chink in the armor, any weakness to exploit, deflate, or defeat your child, God's champion.

A Champion's Cautionary Tale

Think for a moment of what happened to that mighty champion for God, Samson. The story is found in Judges 13–16. Samson was a leader who ruled in Israel for 20 years. More than a leader, this guy was a warrior. He killed a thousand men with the jawbone of a donkey (I can't even visualize that kind of battle). His strength was legendary and his life is a cautionary tale of what happens when you focus on one part of yourself — the physical — and neglect your emotional, intellectual, and spiritual maturity. Granted, through his great strength God was able to use his life, but I can't help but wonder how much more Samson could have accomplished if he'd been a whole champion, instead of a partial one.

I encourage you to take a break right now and read Samson's story from his birth to his death. It's just four chapters long and reads like a Hollywood script. Before Hollywood's disaffection with most things biblical, there were movies made of Samson's life. It's an exciting story, with adventure, battles, and romance. Judges tells the tale of a physically impressive man, able to accomplish feats of muscular prowess, whose very birth was announced by an angel. It's also the tale of a man who, sidetracked by one gift, failed to develop the others.

Samson was physically developed but emotionally immature. Just look at his relationships with women. In fact, the woman who brought about his downfall was actually number three (the first being a Philistine wife, whom Samson wasn't supposed to marry in the first place by a decree of God but did anyway because he liked how she looked, and the second was a prostitute — not a great track record). In some ways, this third woman is as famous as Samson and is forever linked with him. When you think of the story of Samson, don't you automatically think of Samson *and Delilah*? Samson is forever linked with Delilah because in relationships he went for surface over substance.

He not only had trouble controlling his own emotions, he wasn't able to read the thoughts and emotions of others. Delilah was able to play his emotions like a harp, while all the time keeping a tight rein on her own. She knew what she wanted to accomplish — finding out the secret to his great strength — and knew just how to read his emotional states, to punch his buttons, to gain her desired result. Samson either didn't know or didn't care how his wife was playing him.

Samson was physically developed but intellectually stunted. He didn't develop his intellect or use the intellect he had for God. Just look at how Delilah tricked him into revealing the secret of his strength. It's not like she asked him one day and he inadvertently told her, not realizing why that would be a bad idea. Delilah laid a trap for him a total of four times, each time trying to trick him into revealing the secret. I could understand how you might misread things the first time, but *four* times? All the evidence was there to point to her treachery, but Samson either didn't or wouldn't put two and two together. This intellectual oversight ended up costing him his actual sight and his freedom, for when the trap was sprung, Samson was literally blinded and thrown into prison.

Samson was physically strong but spiritually weak. To me, one of the saddest parts of this story is how Samson valued and worked on his relationship with others while neglecting his relationship with God. He was willing to go to great lengths to obtain the relationships he wanted from the women in his life, going out of his way to have women he shouldn't. He was willing to go to great lengths to avenge what he felt were slights in his relationships by others, as when he fought against his wife's relatives at his wedding. It seems like the only relationships that produced passion were earthly ones; he just didn't seem to value his spiritual relationship with God. This is especially striking, considering the times in Samson's life when he was privileged to be filled with God's Spirit to accomplish some amazing feat. God had been right there with him, even prior to birth, articulating the future he had laid out for Samson. Maybe he just took God's intervention in his life for granted. I wonder if he — deep down — liked the rewards of that relationship more than the relationship itself. The relationship with God should be our reward, not what He gives us as a result of that relationship. That's like saying to our earthly father, "I only love you for the things you give me." Reading about parts of Samson's life, I get the impression that's just how he felt.

Samson was a warrior, a champion for God, but his life could have been much more rich and fulfilling if it hadn't been so one-sided. His emotional immaturity resulted in harmful relationships. His intellectual immaturity resulted in betrayal. His spiritual immaturity resulted in physical disfigurement and death. Of course, God in His mercy stayed with Samson even when Samson didn't stay close to God. Even with a partial champion, God was able to avenge himself against the evil of the Philistines.

Now, why bring up this story about Samson (and Delilah)? After all, your child is probably not going to slay thousands with the jawbone of a donkey, but God does have in mind battles for your child to face, for Him. So, I bring this up as an illustration of how important it is for the champion under your roof to be molded into a whole-person champion. God gifted Samson with strength, which he used for God, but the enemy was aware of Samson's weaknesses and used devious methods to orchestrate his downfall.

For our champions to be equipped in all areas, to present in the various arenas of life, they need to develop in a whole-person way. After all, arenas come in a variety of forms, especially as a child grows. Champions, therefore, need to be multi-layered, which is often not the way the world views a champion. It's not enough for someone just to be strong or smart — all parts of the person need development.

A Whole-Person Champion

Now, some may think of a champion, especially a sports champion, as someone who is all brawn and no brain. This may be true of Samson, but it is certainly not true of many of the champions I've known in my life. Take, for example, a champion for God who happens to attend church with my family. He doesn't use a donkey's jawbone; he uses a pigskin. I've mentioned him before. His name is Shaun, and he lives for God every day of his life. Courageous, he never fails to use an opportunity to tell others about God or to give God credit for the remarkable blessings that happen in his life. He works hard and trains to be the very best he can be and inspires others to do the same. While his body is strong, so is his mind, as he is an articulate witness to God's power in his life. I can attest to his spiritual maturity and am amazed at how he keeps his emotional balance through the challenges of his life. This is a multi-dimensional champion, a whole-person champion, who truly loves God with all his heart, soul, mind, and strength.

Shaun is God's champion on spiritual battlefields. He's also known as a champion on an earthly field — in fact, he was recently named the Most Valuable Player for the National Football League. Shaun's last name is Alexander and he's the premier running back for the Seattle Seahawks. In order for him to perform at peak levels — for God and on the athletic field — he has developed his whole person — his emotional, spiritual, intellectual, and physical self. Shaun, even with his athletic gifts, doesn't allow himself to short-change the other parts of his life. He keeps himself in whole-person balance.

Balancing the Emotional Self

As a parent, I'm sometimes amazed at the depth of emotion displayed by my children. The oldest, Gregg, is a textbook on joy when he greets my mother — his grandmother — after a long absence. I don't have to see his face to know how he feels, as he buries himself deep in her arms his whole body just radiates joy at being with her again. Like any three-year old, Benjamin gives new meaning to the word *disappointment* when thwarted in his earnest desire for something. His emotional response overwhelms every part of that little body. Rather than become concerned, I'm in awe of how God is going to use that energy! Both of my boys, like your own kids, are emotional beings and can become supercharged.

Emotions, both positive and negative, are potent energy, and as a therapist I've seen that energy harnessed for incredible good and loosed for unspeakable harm. Emotions, to continue the energy analogy, are like electrical current; they're necessary to keep life powered. After all, someone with no visible display of emotion is considered stoic, lifeless. Can you imagine a life with no joy, no happiness, no wonder? Or a life without sadness, frustration, or even grief, for that matter? No, your life needs an emotional component, but emotions are like current — too little can produce deadness and too much can blow circuits and cause fires.

Our children need to learn how to harness and handle this powerful force in their lives. This emotional current that runs through your child, God's champion, can energize and empower, or it can short-circuit a God-ordained destiny. Our children need to learn to *recognize* and *regulate* their own emotions, and *read* and *respond* to the emotions of others.

The Crucible of Family

Once again, it is in the crucible of family that children learn how to handle their emotions and the emotions of others. Daniel Goleman, in his important book entitled *Emotional Intelligence*, says this: "Family life is our first school for emotional learning; in this intimate cauldron we learn how to feel about ourselves and how others will react to our feelings; how to think about these feelings and what choices we have in reacting; how to read and express hopes and fears."[1] Childhood is an emotional learning curve and one of our primary functions as parents is to help our children deal with their God-given emotions. We want our kids to develop emotional balance — where our children neither deny their emotions nor are burned up by them. Like any power, they need to learn to harness their emotions — for good. When their emotions are properly harnessed, they can respond appropriately to the emotions of others. The school is the family and as the parent, you're the teacher. So, how do we help our children deal with these volatile, varied emotions?

The Transformer of Love

If our emotions are a powerful current, we need a transformer. By transformer, I don't mean those toys that go from one shape to another. Instead, I mean those boxes that hang on power poles. Transformers are also found outside of large buildings and industrial sites. Transformers take the incredible power surging through the utility lines and modify it so it matches the voltage needed for the situation. Most small businesses and residences use 110 volts to power our appliances and gadgets. Large manufacturing plants can use thousands of volts in their industrial machinery, but even they will have an on-site transformer that makes sure the right amount of voltage is passed along, to either the little copier in the office or the big processor on the shop floor. Different situations and different end uses require differing amounts of voltage. It takes a transformer to handle all those differences, to make sure that the right amount of voltage is applied to any given device.

Likewise, our children need to know how to make sure that the right type and amount of emotion is being applied to any given situation. Too little creates an apathetic, pale response to life, and too much creates volcanic, caustic emotional states. So, how does your child — or any of us, for that matter — know how to respond in just the right way to the myriad emotional cues and demands we encounter in our daily lives? Rather than try to go into every possible emotion situation potentially experienced by your child, I'd like to suggest that you instead focus on teaching your child how to channel all of them through a single emotion. If I was to try to create some sort of a visual chart, with all the potential combinations of emotions, it would probably take up an entire wall. After all, on any given day, your child can experience happiness, anxiousness, joy, disappointment, frustration, elation, satisfaction, relief, anger, or fear. Frankly, that's how my day can go! It seems to me that God says there's one universal emotional transformer that can help your child stay emotionally balanced as he or she grows into adulthood. When our complex emotional lives are routed through this transformer, we have power to perform and wisdom to respond. That transformer is love.

The Bible has a lot to say about love. The word is used in almost 700 places in Scripture. Love is an amazing entity. It is both emotional and intellectual; it is both a feeling and a decision. It is both a spiritual gift from God and a spiritual response from us. Love is a response and a reaction. Love truly has it all! I believe love's complexity comes from this statement in Scripture: "God is love" (1 John 4:8). Perhaps love is able to unfold to meet our every emotional demand because it holds the essence of God himself. Only something so powerful, so pure, could have the ability to transform our volatile emotional states into an appropriate, loving response.

Since love is so multi-dimensional, it's vital that God's champions understand how it takes everyday human situations and reacts. If our children know what love does, they can do likewise. Here is what that beautiful love passage in 1 Corinthians 13:4–8 says: *"Love is patient, love is kind. It does not envy, it does not boast, it is not proud. It is not rude, it is not self-seeking, it is not easily angered, it keeps no record of wrongs. Love does not delight in evil but rejoices with the truth. It always protects, always trusts, always hopes, always perseveres. Love never fails."*

My goal as a parent is to help my children learn to *recognize* and *regulate* their own emotions, and *read* and *respond* to the emotions of others. Because I'm human and fallible, I need help to do this. By using a template of love, I'm able to bring God's power and wisdom to this task. If love is to be the template, how is it to be applied? Well, we know that the Bible teaches we are to love God; we've seen that from Mark 12:30. The very next verse in Mark says to "love your neighbor as yourself." We are to love God, but we are also to extend that love to our neighbors and to ourselves.

I want my children to love themselves. When children learn to love themselves, they are given the security of exploring who they are. They are able to risk personal discovery and have the support needed to learn to recognize their emotions. They learn to understand their emotional makeup. Once they *recognize* their emotions for what they are, they can begin to place those emotions under control. They are able to *regulate* their own emotional responses in a way that neither devalues who they are for having those emotions nor exploits emotional intensity. Mark 12:31 teaches that in whatever capacity children love self, they will have the same capacity to love others.

Sometimes I feel Christian parents put a great deal of emphasis on loving God and loving others. Of course, this is vital! However, please don't hinder your child's emotional development by not helping your child learn to love him or herself. A child who doesn't love self is a blinded champion. We are to see ourselves as God does, and He clearly finds us lovable. If children do not have a solid image of themselves, based in love, they will have difficulty garnering the motivation and courage to venture out as champions for God. Instead, they will seek endless blind alleys looking for love, unable to recognize it in themselves, unable to extend it to others.

Again, love is the full circle. Our children need to learn to love themselves and they need to learn to extend that love to others. The Bible calls these others "neighbors" in Mark 12:31. It also calls these others by another name — "enemies." Our champions need to realize they are to love their enemies (Matt. 5:44). Who are their "enemies"? Often, it's their neighbors; sometimes, it might even be you. When children learn to love others, they are empathetic. Instead of reacting to others, they learn to respond by reading the emotional states of others. They're able to respond in a loving way to the people around them. Love becomes the controlling authority, not how they are feeling. This is emotional maturity. With this maturity, they are able to apply the correct emotional response to any given situation. They are emotionally buoyant and can land on their feet if their buttons are pushed. They are emotionally intelligent and can discern the motives and desires behind the actions of others. In this way they can respond appropriately, especially when it requires they protect themselves against others.

Okay, let's take it down to the real world. When I take a look at all those things listed in the characteristics of love in 1 Corinthians 13, I could think, *How am I ever going to pull that off?* It seems too big of a thing. How am I going to teach my children to be patient and kind? To refrain from envying what others have? To avoid boasting about themselves and their own accomplishments? To never act rudely or in a self-serving manner? To only get angry when it's right to do so? To somehow avoid the human tendency to keep spreadsheets on the faults of others? To keep themselves from aligning with evil and stay firmly on the side of truth? To always protect, hope, trust, and persevere in their lives? How can I do all that for them when I can't even do all that for myself? Help!

Then I ask myself, "Do you love your children?" Of course, I answer "yes!" "Can I help my children, day by day, situation by situation, to be more loving?" "Yes!" I can extend more love to my children because my children have given me more love. My children have opened up in me an unexpected storehouse of love; the least I can do is return the incredible favor. You can do the same for your children; help your children to learn how to love themselves and each other. Out of this, your family will become the school house when love is taught, modeled, discussed and tried out. Your children will learn to channel their emotional lives through the transformer of love, and God will provide the right energy to power their emotional lives.

Well-Rounded Emotions

I want my children to experience a wide range of emotions. My job as a parent isn't to shield them from emotions. My children are not dolls with permanent, painted smiles on their faces. Sure, it's great when my children experience joy and happiness, but I also want them to be frustrated and sad. Frustration can motivate you to find a different way of doing things. Sadness is completely appropriate, for example, when experiencing sin. If my children don't experience a wide range of emotions while they are young and under my tutelage, how will they know how to handle them after they're grown?

Because emotions are so powerful, some of us can tend to either shy away from them as unreliable or use them as a blowtorch. I've seen how damaging it is for children to grow up with a distant, unresponsive parent whose own emotional fear sentences their children to a cold, analytic relationship. I've also seen parents who blow up like a volcano with little warning and even less thought beyond their need to vent. As Daniel Goleman says, our family is the first school for emotions and we are our children's first teachers.

Because of this, we need to be aware of how we respond to emotions — both our own and our children's. (The "Training Ground" section at the end of this chapter will help you to think about the emotional lessons you're teaching your children right now.) I want to be well-rounded myself, with an emotional range that fits the person and place. Emotions are not one-size-fits-all. If we have emotional depth, our children will learn from us.

Just as it's important not to respond one-size-fits-all emotionally, it's important to be aware of the emotional differences in our children — just as they are different on the outside, they are different emotionally on the inside. Get to know your child's emotional "flavor." Even though my children are young, I can already see a great deal about their emotional makeup. Gregg, though serious, is a very sensitive child. If I'm not careful, he can miss out on the joy of certain situations because of his concern over what might happen. Impulsive little Benjamin recovers emotionally much more quickly. Like one of those dolls with a rounded base, when he gets knocked down he tends to pop right back up. Gregg is steady but cautious. Benjamin is impulsive but resilient. They are different people, with different emotional tendencies.

Because I know my children's emotional makeup, I can assist them in stretching emotionally in ways that don't come naturally. If I simply leave them to their own personalities, they could become one-sided emotionally. How do I know this? I've spent countless hours with adults who never developed emotional depth and range. Instead, they react to most situations with limited emotional response. One always assumes the worst of self and cowers in fear. Another always assumes the worst of others and retaliates in anger. Another walls off emotionally to the point it's difficult for relationships to take root. Another is so emotionally intense others feel suffocated.

As a parent, I need to help my children explore the circumstances around emotion and learn to choose from different avenues of expression. This doesn't mean they won't naturally react initially in a certain way; they're still hard-wired with certain traits. But I can teach them how to look at what they are doing, at what others are doing, and begin to make choices about how to respond rather than simply react. Children tend to react to things; as adults, we learn to respond. This intentionality is a hallmark of maturity. It's also the hallmark of an emotionally balanced champion.

The Six Questions of Emotions

Because of my line of work, I'm constantly evaluating what effect my actions and words have on my children. One thing I don't ever want to convey is that strong emotions are wrong or bad. They're not. But emotions don't take place in a vacuum. They have a context. When you understand the emotion within the context of the circumstance, you begin to respond instead of react. Like any situation, it's always good to ask the following six questions to get to the bottom of things — What, Why, When, Where, How, and Who. If the emotional response makes sense given the circumstances, then it's appropriate. As adults, we've learned (or should have learned) to ask ourselves the following questions when experiencing our emotions:

- *What emotion am I really feeling?* This can be tricky because often we react in anger when we're really fearful. Or we express frustration when we're really grieving.

- *Why am I feeling this way?* What are the real reasons? If I feel satisfaction when a co-worker is chastised, is it because I'm really concerned about the company or because I think their demotion means my elevation? I need to know who I am and where my feelings come from. Only when I know myself can I judge the source of my emotion.

- *Is this a good "when" for the emotion?* In other words, would a different time be better? How many of us have made the mistake of launching into a spirited complaint about our spouse after we haven't seen each other all day? What we're feeling may be completely appropriate given the situation, but if our timing is wrong, it's not going to be received well. Waiting for the right "when" is a form of delayed gratification. Are we able to delay closure on an emotion until a more appropriate time?

- *Where am I?* Emotional responses and interactions tend to gain attention. I guarantee, in a crowded room of people, if a couple is engaged in a "serious" discussion, people notice. If you start laughing during a somber event, those around take note. Emotions have a place. Where is the right place for this emotion?

- *How am I expressing this emotion?* Disappointment, for example, is a valid emotion, but not when screaming, threatening, or physicality is involved. There is a way to let your feelings be known and it doesn't include abusive behavior.

- *Who am I really reacting to?* One of the hardest things to learn is how to figure out who is behind our emotional responses. It's the old joke about the boss who yells at the employee, who yells at the spouse, who yells at the kid, who kicks the dog, who chases the cat. It's so important, when expressing emotion, to make sure it's directed toward the appropriate person.

So, how does this work with our kids? We can teach them to evaluate their reactions and learn to respond to situations. Here's an example of how this could work. This happened to me recently so I'm speaking from personal experience here. We were up skiing in the mountains this winter and Gregg refused to wear his helmet. It was clearly explained that he had to wear the helmet to begin to ski but he vehemently refused. It took me a minute to figure out what was going on:

- *What* — Gregg was refusing to follow my instructions to put on his helmet before skiing.

- *Why* — He said the helmet was uncomfortable and he didn't want to wear it.

- *When* — We were getting ready to start skiing and the helmet was the last piece of equipment to be put on.

- *Where* — At the top of a snowy hill, with all sorts of people around!

- *How* — Digging his heels in and refusing to obey my (calm) requests.

- *Who* — Gregg and me — and a host of strangers who were milling around watching.

It soon became apparent that Gregg was focusing on the wrong aspect of the helmet. In his mind the most important thing about the helmet was its lack of comfort. I mean, a ski helmet doesn't feel like a ball cap or a soft, wool hat. The helmet is still kind of foreign and it takes some getting used to. After all, he's still fairly young and hasn't skied that often. Gregg focused on how the helmet felt, not on what the helmet does.

To respond to his emotional outburst, I needed to explain to him again how the helmet was there for his protection, so he could ski without worrying about falling and hitting his head. We talked about how he wears a helmet when he rides his bike for the same reason. He likes to wear his bike helmet; he thinks it's cool. He just needed to think of his ski helmet like his bike helmet. I needed to make sure there wasn't something wrong with the helmet. That it didn't pinch anywhere or there wasn't a protrusion poking him. I could have just put my foot down, yelled at him to put on the helmet or he couldn't go skiing. I've seen it happen before, but I love my son and recognized there was a reason he was refusing. I took the time to figure out what was really wrong, devise an appropriate response, and deliver that response in a loving way. Gregg learned more that day than just about skiing or how helmets protect you. We may have been on the top of a mountain but we were really in the school — the schoolhouse Daniel Goleman spoke about. The lesson that day was how to respond instead of react to another person's emotions.

Emotional Intelligence

Daniel Goleman coined the phrase "emotional intelligence" for a person's ability to understand their own emotional responses and those of others. He says on the cover of his book, "It can matter more than IQ." People with emotional intelligence are able to function in this world because they maneuver the emotional shoals of human relationships. They have the ability to motivate people to feel better about themselves, about life. I think that's a quality God also finds valuable. God does not want champions who are unprepared to handle their own emotions or unable to read the emotions of others. He wants champions who are emotional, yet self-controlled, who can be responsive to other people in a loving, appropriate way.

Let's go back for a moment and revisit Samson. For all his physical strength, Samson was unprepared for the type of battle Delilah engaged in. Hers was an emotional battle. If Samson had been emotionally intelligent, he would have discerned Delilah's actions and motives. He would have read her true feelings for him. Instead, he remained emotionally uncontrolled and clueless. Delilah was able to goad him into irritation and anger so he revealed his secret to her. She was able to keep her greed and disdain for him hidden. He neither controlled himself nor understood her and it proved his undoing.

Love is the basis for emotional intelligence. Through love, you exhibit the emotional attributes needed to respond intentionally to situations instead of reacting to them. As you become more loving, you're able to discern when others are not. You constantly evaluate your behavior and the behavior of others through the filter of love. This is the legacy you want to pass on to your children.

Now, the wonderful thing is, you don't have to be perfect at this, because love includes forgiveness. Remember, love doesn't keep a record of wrongs and it always hopes. One of the most poignant lessons in love you can give to your child is to ask your child for forgiveness when needed (if an opportunity to do this hasn't happened yet, believe me, it will — and soon!). Children need to experience forgiveness in its various facets. They need to know what it feels like to receive it and they need to know what it feels like to give it.

Don't be afraid to express emotions yourself. What you model, you teach. What you teach, they learn. Have your emotions and handle them appropriately and your children will see how it's done. Respond lovingly to their emotions and your children will learn love in action.

Training Ground

Handling emotions well is a vital lesson for your champion. I couldn't begin to count the number of people whose plans for life were short-circuited by their inability to channel the flow of their emotions or were unprepared to understand the emotions of others. It's not an easy, say-it-once kind of thing; it's a live-it-daily kind of thing. Your child is your emotional apprentice. The task is so big, the only way to accomplish it is over time, by first carefully allowing them to observe you, then by letting them try out what they're learning. Oh, and remember the first aspect of love from First Corinthians — it is patience.

So, what is your child learning about emotions from you? Before we finish this chapter, I want you to make an honest appraisal of your own heart. Think about these questions as they relate to you and your family:

- What are the primary emotions my child experiences from me?

- How do I respond to my child's various emotional states?

- Are emotions accepted in my house or are they rejected?

- Am I the only one in my house allowed to show emotions?

- Is there more joy expressed in my house than anger?

- Is there more excitement than irritation?

- Is forgiveness easy to give and receive?

- In the realm of relationships, what are the top three lessons my life is teaching my child? Are these the ones I'd choose, if I could make changes?

- What changes in my emotions do I need to make?

- Thinking about each of my children, what are his or her emotional strengths?

- What are his or her emotional challenges?

- Do my child and I share similar emotional challenges?

As human beings, we're flawed; we know that. We react instead of respond. In order to help you in the responding department, I want you to do a little more memorizing. I want you to memorize the 1 Corinthians 13 passage. Here it is again: *"Love is patient, love is kind. It does not envy, it does not boast, it is not proud. It is not rude, it is not self-seeking, it is not easily angered, it keeps no record of wrongs. Love does not delight in evil but rejoices with the truth. It always protects, always trusts, always hopes, always perseveres. Love never fails"* (1 Cor: 4–8).

More and more, these must become your responses:

- For your child to be patient, you must be patient.

- For your child to be kind, you must show kindness to those around you, especially your family.

- For your child to reject the trap of envy, you must take joy in the accomplishments of others.

- For your child to avoid being a braggart, you must temper your own accomplishments with humility.

- For your child to have a healthy view of self, you must teach that God is the source of our victories.

- For your child to act politely, you must watch your speech and actions toward others.

- For your child to have empathy, you need to place others' needs above your own.

- For your child to learn restraint, you must avoid rage and bitterness.

- For your child to learn forgiveness, you must put the past behind you.

- For your child to reject evil, you must embrace good at every turn.

- For your child to mature, you must demonstrate what maturity looks like — protecting the weak, trusting the good, hoping for tomorrow, and persevering through today.

Love your child and you won't fail.

> *Father, help me! I love my child so much but I am over-*
> *whelmed at the thought of trying to do everything right. Fill*
> *up my holes. Finish my sentences. Temper my speech. Open my*
> *mouth when needed and shut it when necessary. I recognize*
> *for my child to be emotionally healthy and balanced, I need to*
> *do my very best to emulate Your love. I thank You that You've*
> *shown me so much about love through my children. Continue*
> *to show me how I can love my children back each day. Help*
> *me not to fail; I know You won't.*

Endnote

1. Daniel Goleman, *Emotional Intelligence* (New York: Bantam Books, 1995), p. 189–190.

Chapter 7

Spiritual
Depth

*Train a child in the way he should go, and when he is old
he will not turn from it* (Prov. 22:6).

I love sports. I love to play them and I love to watch them. In the fall, we're at Qwest Field to watch our friend, Shaun, and the Seattle Seahawks on the football field. In the winter, I take my kids to Seattle SuperSonics basketball games, and in the spring and summer we're at Safeco, rooting on the Mariners in baseball. We go every chance we get. It is one of the great joys in life to share my passion for sports with my kids. Each game is like a little community event, when people of like mind come together to devote time, energy, and enthusiasm to the team, to the sport.

I want them to learn not only know how to watch sports but how to get in there and play, as well. So I take my kids to games but I also take them to the park. There, we practice shooting hoops or throwing Frisbees or catching and hitting a ball. We'll run up and down hills, chasing each other. They've got a lot of energy and this is a great way to channel it. I remember doing this with my own dad and it just seems right to do it with my kids.

Now Benjamin is still a little young for organized sports, being three. For him, it's just as fun running the bases backwards as forward. He just likes throwing the ball up in the air; he doesn't care if it goes in the basket. Gregg, however, is old enough for baseball and he's joined a local team. The other day we were out at the park, practicing his hitting. I was throwing him the ball and letting him get the feel of how to watch its trajectory, how to swing the bat, and what it feels like to make good contact with the ball. He was trying really hard to hit it and I was trying just as hard to pitch it so he *could* hit it! I got ready to pitch the ball and told him to be ready because I was going to throw a fast one. All of a sudden, he stopped. He put the bat down and I watched him bow his head and clasp his hands in prayer. He stayed that way for a few seconds, then hoisted the bat back up over his shoulder and announced, "Okay, Dad, now I'm ready." Saying a quick prayer myself, I threw the ball over the plate and heard a sharp, satisfying "crack!" A line drive down the third-base line. It doesn't get much better than that!

Or does it? What Gregg did the other day at the park caused me to think. First, I realized Gregg doesn't consider his relationship with God confined to a church building. When he was apprehensive about the ball I was going to pitch, Gregg stopped and talked to God about it. Standing at home plate is as natural a place to pray for Gregg as sitting in a church pew or kneeling in front of his bed at night. In Gregg's mind, God is everywhere, so prayer is everywhere. Second, it reminded me to put as much time, energy, and devotion into passing along my spiritual legacy to my son as I am passing along my sports legacy.

The bedrock foundation of the life of a child should be spiritual development and a growing relationship and belief in God and Christ. I don't want my children to have just a surface belief in and knowledge of God. Just saying, "I believe in God," is not the hallmark of a spiritual champion. James 2:19 says "You believe that there is one God. Good! Even the demons believe that — and shudder." Luke 8:27–29 tells the story of a demon-possessed man who identified Christ as "Jesus, Son of the Most High God." Even demons believe and know, and that's not enough. You don't want your children to have a spiritual depth no deeper than demons!

Spiritual Maturity

Sadly, a surface depth is one that many parents find acceptable. They will vaguely communicate a general belief in the presence of God and show a moderate knowledge of Christ. Maybe that's all they received from their own parents or maybe they are spiritually shallow themselves. Our children, as God's champions, need more. They need to plumb the depths of spiritual understanding and connection to become spiritually mature.

The Bible talks about developing spiritual maturity. In James 1:4, maturity is compared with being "complete, not lacking anything." This is both a statement and a promise. God promises that if we work toward maturity in spirit, he will make us complete, not lacking anything. This promise is extended to me, to you, and to our children.

Seeds 101

So, how do we help our children gain spiritual maturity? The first is to encourage a love for God's Word. Let's look at a great story Jesus tells in Luke 8 about a sower of seeds. Now, for those of you who weren't raised in the farm country of Idaho, like I was, a sower is someone who spreads seed around so it can grow and be harvested. Luke 8:5 starts out: "A farmer went out to sow his seed. As he was scattering the seed, some fell along the path; it was trampled on, and the birds of the air ate it up. Some fell on rock, and when it came up, the seeds withered because they had no moisture. Other seed fell among thorns, which grew up with it and choked the plant. Still other seed fell on good soil. It came up and yielded a crop, a hundred times more than was sown" (Luke 8:5–8).

Jesus often used commonplace, understandable illustrations of earthly situations to connect to deeper spiritual truths. Those He was speaking to understood completely what happened if you scattered seed in good and bad places. They'd seen it first-hand in their own lives. This was Seeds 101, and the seeds represented God's Word. Jesus goes on to explain exactly what He meant by this parable, something I'm extremely grateful for. Verses 11–15 continue: "This is the meaning of the parable: The seed is the word of God. Those along the path are the ones who hear, and then the devil comes and takes away the word from their hearts, so that they may not believe and be saved. Those on the rock are the ones who receive the word with joy when they hear it, but they have no root. They believe for a while, but in the time of testing they fall away. The seed that fell among thorns stands for those who hear, but as they go on their way they are choked by life's worries, riches, and pleasures, and they do not mature. But the seed on good soil stands for those with a noble and good heart, who hear the word, retain it, and by persevering produce a crop."

This parable is a warning and a promise. It's a warning to parents what will happen if their children aren't prepared to receive the Word of God. Some parents believe it's enough to just scatter the seed. They think, "I'll expose my children to religion and then it's up to them whether or not they believe." These parents do nothing to amend the soil, to enrich it and prepare it with the composition and nutrients it needs to be able to grow the seed.

Just because you scatter the seed — or expose your children to the word — it doesn't automatically mean a spiritual harvest in your child. Why? Look at the first example — that soil was so hard and packed down, the seed wasn't even able to get below the surface! Left exposed to the elements, people stepped on it and birds ate it. It never had a chance. It is possible to harden our children; to compact them down with criticism and negativity, to leave them defenseless to the world and allow people to just walk all over them. The more people trample our children, over a long enough period of time, the hearts of our children will become well-worn paths of cracked, hard dirt. Ideas of love, kindness, gratitude, empathy, and compassion just won't be able to penetrate. Instead, even if they are exposed to these truths from God, they won't sink down into their hearts. Instead, they'll just skitter along the surface, to be crushed when our children get walked on or plucked up by the next circumstance that comes swooping down in their lives.

We certainly don't want our children to be hard and impenetrable when it comes to God's Word. Hopefully, that's not your situation. What about where the soil of our children has some nourishment, some dirt to take root in, but is so full of rocks, it can't hold any moisture? I believe this happens when God is included as just a small part of our lives. There are too many large, worldly rocks worked into our spiritual soul, that when the Word sprouts and takes root, there just isn't enough there to sustain the growth through the tough times. Often these times manifest themselves during the furnace known as adolescence. Jesus says this happens during the inevitable time of testing. Each one of us has our faith tested, and God wants His Word planted into good, rich soil so that when the conditions for faith on the outside are less than optimum, we have enough living water stored inside us to carry us through.

The next example is one I really have to confess to needing help with. I need help to discern the thorns that are growing up in my child's life and heart. These thorns are "life's worries, riches, and pleasures." When they choke out my child's ability to receive God's Word, my child will not mature.

This is where it is so easy to get off track as a parent. Our children observe how we deal with the world. If our preoccupation in life is with worry, riches, or pleasure, we're allowing thorns to grow up around our children. What do I worry about? About what am I concerned? And what does that tell my child about what I value? Is my life consumed with the acquisition of wealth and "riches"? Do I demonstrate with my time and energy what I value in this world? How about pleasure? Am I too busy with my hobbies and enjoyments to spend time with God, with other Christians, and in the Word?

I so want my child to have "a noble and good heart, who hear the word, retain it, and by persevering produce a crop." In order to help them in any way I can, I need to make sure the soil they take from my home is good and rich and deep. I need to help them begin today to be working and amending their soil. My family soil extends only so far; my children need their own rich, deep soil to retain the Word and persevere.

Soil Enrichment

I spoke earlier about how much fun it is to share my love of sports with my children. As great as that is, it's just a shadow of how much joy I receive from sharing my love of God. Yes, I love to jump up and down with my family and yell and cheer on the team, whether it's Gregg's little baseball team or the Seahawks. We hug each other, smile, and laugh out loud, whenever there's a great play. Whooping and hollering, we love to generally make a spectacle of ourselves, along with everyone else around us. Remember how I said at the beginning of this chapter that it's kind of like a community event?

I think church is like that, too. Only the joy and camaraderie gained through worshiping and praising together lasts so much longer than a sporting event. I need to make sure I'm taking advantage of the strength gained within a spiritual community. In this way, it's not just my family enriching our soil; it's the whole faith community enriching each other. This is why LaFon and I are committed to a local congregation. We attend every time we're able. We make it a priority in our family. Church isn't something we go to if there's nothing else better to do. Instead, we recognize going to church as one of the most important things we do as a family, where a great deal of soil enrichment takes place. Hebrews 10:24–25 talks about the enrichment of fellowship, saying, "And let us consider how we may spur one another on towards love and good deeds. Let us not give up meeting together, as some are in the habit of doing, but let us encourage one another — all the more as we see the Day approaching." Fellowship is an enriching experience for the soil of my family.

Sunday is the day my family gets together to cheer for God with our spiritual family. This commitment on our part yields healthier soil. There are days when I don't really have a lot to give and I need other Christians to supply my lack. This will also be true of my children, as they get older. I want them to learn to seek out a faith community whenever they end up in this world, to provide enrichment for others and to be enriched themselves.

Taking the Power Out of the Pew

What I love about Gregg's story is how he thought it was perfectly appropriate to stop in the middle of a leisure activity in a public park and pray. He's young enough still not to realize that some people feel that faith should be placed in a box, opened only at certain times and in certain places. Gregg, with his batter's prayer, is beginning to internalize Paul's admonition to "pray without ceasing" (1 Thess. 5:17). God isn't someone we just agree to meet on Sunday mornings at church. Should we expect God to show up on Sunday? You bet! But He is not confined to such a limited place and time. God is infinite, everywhere, and constantly available to our children.

I want my children to get used to having Jesus as their best friend. I want them to be able to visualize and internalize His constant presence in their lives. We are not alone; Jesus promised us in Hebrews 13:5 ". . . God has said, 'Never will I leave you; never will I forsake you.' " He also promised in Matthew 28:20: "And surely I am with you always, even to the very end of the age." Did you notice the quotation marks there? These are not mere religious principles but actual statements of Jesus. When my children leave my home, whenever that is and in whatever form that takes, I want them to have Jesus with them. I don't want them to think they have to go to some particular place at some particular time to find Him. The power isn't in the pew, it's in the Person.

The Best Book I've Ever Read, and Read Again

I read a lot. I read over 40 different books just in preparation for writing this one. Partly, I wanted to be able to give you the chapter at the back with recommendations and suggestions, as a follow-up to this book. If I'm honest, though, I also read them because I just like to read. What other people think and how they articulate those thoughts is fascinating to me. I love a good story, a great adventure. I read for my writing; I read for work; I read for pleasure. I've also been reading a lot to my kids.

LaFon and I are building up a pretty extensive children's library at our house. Our boys love to go to the book shelves and pick out a book for us to read to them. Soon, Gregg will be reading more and more on his own. Both boys, however, still enjoy being read to. With all of the books they can choose from, there's one book that isn't a choice; it's a standard. We read the Bible to our children. I want them each to develop a love for God's Word. I want them to know God's love revealed in Scripture and God's plan for them revealed in Christ.

The Bible isn't a book you read just once. It's not a book that's the same the second time you read it. Hebrews 4:12 says, "For the word of God is living and active." Because the Bible is God-breathed (2 Tim. 3:16), it is alive with the Spirit of God. Every time I read it, I am changed. I may read a passage one week and learn something, then turn around and read it again the next week and learn something completely new. The Bible is a book of constant discovery. I want my children to learn to love it, rely on it, know it, and trust it.

To help with this, LaFon and I help the boys memorize Scripture, especially passages that make sense to them at their age. I'm not having them memorize Christ's lineage out of Matthew! (That falls under the category of "exasperating" your children!) Rather, we have them memorize simple statements about God's love for them and His promises to them. A great way to do this is to get one of those small, devotional calendars. Often, they will have simple, one-sentence statements each day. Even if your child isn't at the age to memorize, you can still talk about each statement and help your child understand how it applies to him or her. You can develop anticipation of God's Word through an activity such as this. Wouldn't it be great for your child to want to know what God has to say each and every day?

Talking to God

Children don't seem to have any trouble talking to God. Gregg sure didn't at the park. It was natural for him to want God right there with him when he hit the ball. This natural communication with God is called prayer, but it's really a conversation. We talk to God and He talks to us. Like in any relationship, sometimes we do all the talking and sometimes we need to just be quiet and listen. I want my children to have a personal relationship with Jesus, where talking and listening is a natural component. I want talking with Jesus to be as normal and natural as talking with me.

Prayer is where their faith in God becomes personal. First, a young child hears a parent praying about them and for them. As they get older, the child begins to form his or her own prayers, using yours as an example. There will come a time when your child's prayers will be exclusively between him or her and God. This is their individual relationship with God. I can support it but I can't mandate it. Neither can you. You can point the way but you cannot conduct your child's prayer life. You can, however, support your child's prayer life. Your child needs to be given the tools to learn to pray in all circumstances.

Does your child just hear you pray at the table over food? Or when you're called on at church? Do they hear you stop and pray during a difficult situation? Again, children take their lead from their parents and the adults around them. If prayer is a vital, integral part of your life, your child will see it and emulate it. You'll be watching a love affair take root that will outlast their childhood, into eternity.

Championship Faith

Spiritual development establishes the context through which your child becomes God's champion in this world. God's work is on a spiritual level. Granted, He does a great many things in the physical realm, but His ultimate purposes are spiritual ones. This earth is on a short leash and it's not going to be here forever, but we will, and God's Word will. Isaiah 40:8 and 1 Peter 1:25 clearly says the Word of the Lord lasts forever, and we know we, as humans, are eternal beings. We're going to last and the Word of God is going to last. The things that last are the things worth fighting for. The things that last are what God designs champions for.

If God has in mind battles with spiritual consequences for His champions, it doesn't make sense for those champions not to concentrate a good portion of their time to spiritual training. If God's power to engage in battle is spiritual, it doesn't make sense for His champions to neglect tapping into that power. If God's Spirit is directing the battle, it doesn't make sense for God's champions to be ignorant of their general. If spiritual training was good enough for the Son of God, it's good enough for our sons and daughters.

The Example of Jesus

I've often wondered, reading over the story of Jesus, what it was like to be Him. Was the Spirit always clear to Him or did He have to develop spiritual disciplines? Was He like His cousin, John the Baptist, and have the Spirit just fall on Him one day so He was instantly aware of His purpose? One thing is for sure, even though He was the miraculously conceived, angelically heralded Son of God, He still was brought up like all others in His faith. He wasn't given some sort of a spiritual "pass." He still went to church (synagogue), He still read Scripture, met with God's people, relied on God daily, and spent a good time in prayer. What that means to me is this: If it was good enough for Jesus, it is good enough for Gregg and Benjamin.

I don't believe Jesus could "challenge" out of the spiritual disciplines. You might think that being God, He could just take the spiritual final and avoid taking the class. Why did He have to study the mysteries of creation when He was the One who accomplished them in the first place? Why did He have to read Scripture when He was the fulfillment of it? I think — given His purpose on this earth and who He is — He was meant to take the class so He could show us how it's done.

I have to remember that Jesus is part of God, yes, but He was also fully human. In order to take the class for me, He needed to be like me. This is one of those amazing mysteries of God; I don't have to fully understand it to accept it. Hebrews 4:15 tell us that Jesus was tempted in every way, just like me. Now, to be tempted like me, He has to be like me — fully human — for God cannot be tempted according to James 1:13. Philippians 2 contains a beautiful song about Christ, which says that though He was in very nature God, He humbled himself and became like us. Why would He do such a thing? Yes, out of love — good answer! But also to provide us with an example of how to do what He did — live a life unshackled by sin, obedient to God. Jesus studied God's Word, meditated on God's character, daily renewed His relationship with His Father and talked with Him often. Jesus is God's ultimate champion, and He showed how to live a life dedicated to God's purposes. That's a lesson the champions under my roof need to learn and live.

Training Ground

Your home is basically a Bible boot camp. It's where your little champion for God is being trained for battle. Is your boot camp a state-of-the-art spiritual training facility or do the bunks sag and have weeds grown up the cracks in your training ground? If so, it's time to get your training camp in shape for the important work of spiritually molding your champion. First, you'll need to take stock of your supplies:

- What sort of Bibles do you have? Are they age appropriate?

- Where are the Bibles right now? Out in the open, ready for use, or stashed away in a drawer until the next time you manage to get to church?

- How about supplemental training manuals? Do your children have books, tapes, videos, and DVDs that contain messages and content that is, if not biblically based, at least Bible-friendly?

Second, what about your training schedule?

- Are you out every day as a family engaging in spiritual fitness training?
- Do you pray together several times during the day?
- Do you use the everyday opportunities of life to reinforce spiritual lessons?
- Are your children encouraged and commended for their growing faith?
- Is more attention paid to their social, academic, or athletic accomplishments than their spiritual ones?

Who are the instructors?

- Who has the most influence over your children?
- Are these people reinforcing spiritual lessons and priorities?
- What about "electronic" instructors? What are your children learning from the television, play stations, or computer?
- Are your children getting to church on a regular basis so others can also teach your child about their faith in and reliance upon God and Christ?

Are there times for parades and recognitions?

- Do you make sure to celebrate together as a family the special spiritual milestones, such as:
    graduating to a new Sunday school class
    memorizing a passage of Scripture
    bringing friends to church
    talking to friends about Jesus
    reading through books of the Bible
    demonstrating a spiritual truth

Who is the company commander?

- Who has the most influence over the family? Is it church, work, friends, hobbies, activities?

I encourage you to evaluate the training ground that is your home, from the point of view of raising up a champion for God. Make a list of areas you know have deficiencies. Speak with your spouse or extended family and ask them to do the same. Come up with a list of areas you want to change.

On a piece of paper, place three headings: What — Why — How. The "What" is what needs to be changed in your family. The "Why" is your motivation for doing the necessary things to make that change. The "How" is how you're going to specifically accomplish the needed change. Remember that you don't need to make some changes immediately. Some may require several steps for complete implementation.

Start at a pace that is sustainable. If you've got five significant changes to make, don't do them all at once! Start with what you consider to be the most important. Implement that change and make sure you've done it long enough to establish a pattern. Once the pattern is accepted and working well, implement the next change. If your family is immature spiritually, you'll need to take baby steps — one step at a time, progressing and advancing each day.

Oh, and make the changes as fun and joyful as you can. These are positive steps you're doing! Your family needs to recognize they are positive, even if the only way at first they can see it is in your attitude and love expressed to them.

Spiritual lessons are not meant to be total classroom learning; they are meant also to be "field exercises." So be strategic in how you plan your day and where you introduce the changes. Integrate them into your being and allow them to flow naturally from your own relationship with God. When God becomes such an integral part of who you are, your children and family will be meeting with God naturally, just by being around you! As they see what this means in your own life, they'll seek it out for themselves. Then you're giving what they've asked for instead of pushing what they haven't.

Of all the things I could do with my life, Lord, I can't think of anything more important than helping my children grow to spiritual maturity. I think this would be easier if I was further along myself. I know You want my child to grow and I know You want me to grow. Help us both as we walk this road together. Show me areas I need to change. Provide me opportunities each day to share a precious gem from Your Word with my child. Don't let me slack off or expect someone else to do it for me. I hold onto Your promise, Lord, that if I train my child in Your way, that training will sustain my child into old age. I want my child to grow old. I want my child to grow old knowing You.

Chapter 8

Intelligent Faith

And you, my son Solomon, acknowledge the God of your father, and serve him with wholehearted devotion and with a willing mind, for the LORD searches every heart and understands every motive behind the thoughts. If you seek him, he will be found by you (1 Chron. 28:9).

Always be prepared to give an answer to everyone who asks you to give the reason for the hope that you have (1 Pet. 3:15).

So what shall I do? I will pray with my spirit, but I will also pray with my mind; I will sing with my spirit, but I will also sing with my mind (1 Cor. 14:15).

My two sons, ages six and three, had an interesting conversation the other day while riding in the car together. Gregg turned to his younger brother and asked him, "Do you have Jesus in your heart?"

Benjamin was quick to respond, "Yes, I do!"

"Good," Gregg replied. "Then it means we'll live forever."

I had just witnessed Gregg putting two and two together, spiritually. No casual question, this, "Do you have Jesus in your heart?" Rather, the question came as a result of some internal reasoning on Gregg's part. He loves his brother and wants to be with Benjamin forever and he knows the way to do that is for both of them to have Jesus in their hearts. Gregg knew he did but he just wanted to make sure about Benjamin. When Benjamin replied, "Yes!" that was a good answer.

Gregg is beginning the process of using the intellect God gave him, to reason about spiritual things. Of course, at six, he's using this reasoning to make all kinds of connections to the life around him. That's his job: he's a kid. What I dearly love is that Gregg is not just reasoning about his own six-year-old world, he's also reasoning about eternal truths. God, we know from Romans 1:20, has revealed himself to everyone, and this includes my children. I am not the only person who reveals God to my children. God himself does and my children use the intellect He's given them to reason spiritually. This is intelligent faith.

This intelligent faith, this internal connecting, this putting two and two together, is the mark of a champion of God. It is the mark of all of God's children and an invitation from God himself, who says in Isaiah 1:18, "Come now, let us reason together."

Reason, the intellect, the mind, are very important to God. Faith is not a mindless pursuit. Belief is not a mechanical reaction to God. These are responses, driven by the gift of free will. God does not force us to believe in Him; rather, He offers an invitation to "come and reason." When we accept and draw near to our Creator, we come of our own free will. When He made each one of us, He gave us the reason we need to find Him. In fact, this is a promise of God. As David tells his son, Solomon, "If you seek him, he will be found by you."

To be a whole-person champion, our children need to use their minds to seek after God. They need to use their intellect to reason and understand God's Word and His plan for their lives. This reasoning is sort of like mental exercise. Sometimes it is very difficult and requires the brain to stretch! This is certainly true when trying to wrap your mind about such mysteries as the infinite universe, the triune God, or the concept of eternity!

From learning comes wisdom. The great and wise King Solomon puts it this way in Ecclesiastes 7:25 about his own intellectual pursuit: "So I turned my mind to understand, to investigate and to search out wisdom and the scheme of things." This is what we do, as people. This is also what our children do. In seeking to understand themselves and their world, they investigate, they search out how things fit together and what they mean. This is a valuable and worthwhile endeavor for a champion of God. This endeavor should also be fun, especially for children. After all, children have a great capacity to feel wonder, and who is more wonder-full than God himself?

It never ceases to amaze me how secular people believe that faith is a mindless pursuit. They are sure that, somehow, when we become Christians, we turn our brains in at the door to the church building. As a Ph.D., I've received a fair amount of schooling over my life and I guess you could say I'm a learned man. As much schooling as I've had, there is nothing more complex and intellectually stimulating than my relationship with God. The more I learn about God, the more I realize how much there is left to learn. To me, faith is not a brainless activity. Rather, it is intellectually engaging. When I approach God, I do so with all mental receptors on full power. This is a legacy I want to leave my children.

In order to be mentally prepared for their championship roles for God, our children need to learn to use their brains. There are a variety of ways we can encourage our children in this area. We can help them develop the intellectual gifts God has given them. We can help them to understand and evaluate the world around them. We can guide them to respond to God intellectually. We can teach them to understand and integrate God's Word into their lives.

Intellectual Calisthenics

Training your mind is a lot like training your body. You need to develop a discipline and devote time and energy to doing so. This is something your child is already doing, or will begin shortly — it's called school. From preschool through high school, your child is on an intellectual adventure. There is no reason why you cannot, as a parent, use your child's schooling to help hone and develop the mental tools necessary to develop an intelligent faith.

Many of you, as parents, will choose to enroll your children in a Christian school setting. In this way, spiritual truths will be integrated into your child's educational experience. When learning about biology, for example, your child can see how God's plan for creation is beautifully designed and implemented in the natural world. When studying math, your child can appreciate the ordered nature of God's physical laws. When reviewing important eras in human history, your child can factor in the contributions of people of faith. A biblically based education is certainly a positive for those who are able to provide it.

Some of you will decide to home school your children. I have known many people in my life who have made the tremendous sacrifice to be both parent and teacher to their children. Some families will do this while their children are younger and then move them into a Christian or secular school setting for older grades. Others will home school their children for their entire K-12 education.

I recognize, however, that many of you will not have the means or opportunity to place your children in a Christian school or home school your child. Instead, you will place your child within the public school setting. This does not mean that a secular education cannot be as valuable as a Christian one. I know many parents who choose to place their children — God's champions — in a secular school setting, understanding their children will be salt and light to their community. I truly believe God is able to bless your children in each setting. In fact, the type of educational setting your child is in can be part of the training he or she is receiving from God. Where your child goes to school, and in what setting, is a matter for continued prayer, no matter the age of your child.

There is no auto-pilot, where your child's education is concerned. If you are home schooling your children, you're in charge. This brings its own unique challenges. If your child is in a Christian school, you have the advantage of knowing that the teachers share your religious values and are reinforcing them through the curriculum. If your child is in a public school setting, you have an educational partner in your child's teacher, but you must remain alert and diligent to maintain and provide the necessary spiritual content.

If your child is in a public school, you will need to be aware of what your child is learning and make sure you are available to present God's perspective. Because your child will be presented with secular concepts, you will need to counter with God's view on the matter. This will require a heightened scrutiny, on your part, of your child's curriculum and courses of study.

Through this experience, your child will develop the spiritual reasoning needed for championship arenas. Naturally, even those children who are either home schooled or enrolled in a Christian school will be confronted with secular thoughts, attitudes, and opinions. No matter how much we want to shield our children, we live in this world and our children are exposed to it. For those children in the public school system, however, this exposure will be significant. Vigilance is required, therefore, to safeguard your child against becoming inundated by secular and worldly thought. If your child is in a public school, please recognize that your job as spiritual instructor is a vital component to your child's ability to put spiritual applications onto secular information.

Take heart in the knowledge that God is able to protect and empower your child, no matter what educational setting you choose. The public school system need not be considered adversarial. There are so many dedicated teachers, many of whom are believers, who have chosen to teach as a mission field, to show God's love and compassion for children.

The very act of learning will help your child's intellect to develop and mature. Be actively involved in your child's education. Whether secular or Christian, this is where your child is going to learn about the world and how it works. This is where your child is going to learn how to think and reason through problems, to evaluate situations and hypothesize solutions. For this reason alone, education is extremely important to your budding champion. You never know how God will use what your child learns to help prepare him or her for what lies ahead.

Reason from the Scriptures

In the New Testament, there probably isn't a better example of intelligent faith than the apostle Paul. This is a man who grew up in the Jewish faith, knowing the Scriptures, studying under the great teacher Gamaliel (Acts 22:3). Paul spent his youth and young adulthood in the pursuit of learning. In today's vernacular, Paul could be considered an intellectual.

Paul's life is an illuminating tale in the value of an education. Certainly Paul knew a great many things. He certainly knew the Scriptures. It wasn't until he knew Jesus, however, that his mind and intellect could be used by God. Having a great mind and knowing all manner of subjects is not enough. Our children must know Jesus Christ in order for God to be able to use that knowledge for His glory. Paul's introduction to Jesus is a miraculous event that took place on the road to Damascus, chronicled in Acts 9. Once Paul understood who Jesus is, he was able to harness all of that education and learning for God's purpose. Paul spent the rest of his life preaching and teaching about Christ and God's plan of salvation for all men. Much of what is written in the New Testament comes from the writings of Paul.

An education gives our children knowledge and the ability to reason. It's not enough to leave this to secular endeavors. We must engage our children intellectually in Scripture. Or, put another way, we must view Scripture as *intellectually engaging*. I have heard parents who take the view with their children of "the Bible says it and that settles it!" Their children are browbeaten with Scripture, which becomes a club to hammer in their own sinfulness. When teaching children Scripture, we must not allow our own actions to reduce the fun factor God put into His Word. The story of God's redemption is an adventure! The Bible is an adventure book for kids! It was written to give us hope and lift us up. It was not written to condemn and weigh down. Remember, Revelation has a happy ending!

God fully expects us to ask questions. We should fully expect our children to ask questions, to want to reason out Scripture. We should do more than expect it; we should welcome and encourage it. Questions are not the enemy of learning. God himself invites us to come and reason together. We are supposed to ask questions and be answered by God. We are not robots to merely memorize the Word; we are people, who were made to interact with God through the Word. When I'm reading a section of Scripture with my child, questions do not alarm me. It is the lack of questions that alert me to the possibility that my child just isn't understanding. Questions are good because questions indicate a thinking, reasoning mind. Questions are no problem for a God with all the answers.

Faith and belief are a journey our children take with God. It is not a place we, as parents, can just drop them off. Our children will use the intellect God gave them to investigate whether or not what they are told is true. We should expect our children to become like little Bereans, who are commended in Acts 17:11: "Now the Bereans were of more noble character than the Thessalonians, for they received the message with great eagerness and examined the Scriptures every day to see if what Paul said was true." This group of people received the message but made sure they checked it out. I imagine they asked all kinds of questions. Rather than being chastised for not just accepting Paul's words without examination, they were commended for making sure what they heard was true. When our children question what we tell them, instead of reacting in a hostile way, we should commend them for their desire to seek truth and help point them to the truth in Scripture. Once there, we need to allow them to examine those Scriptures for themselves. In this way, their intellectual investigation will result in a greater faith, an intelligent faith.

The day my children stop asking questions about Scripture is the day they stop learning. Again, their questions don't frighten me; their lack of questions does. When they ask questions, they are engaged in reasoning and this is a very biblical activity.

Whenever Paul went into a new town, he went straight for one place, with one purpose in mind. Acts 17:2 says, "As his custom was, Paul went into the synagogue, and on three Sabbath days he reasoned with them from the scriptures." Our children need to not only know the Scriptures, they need to know how to reason from them. Our children will be confronted with their own questions and the questions of others. They need to be prepared to take what they know from Scripture, understand it, and apply it to the given situation.

Shrewd As Snakes

We often look at our children as little lambs, and they are, but they need to be more. There's an interesting verse in Matthew 10:16, where Jesus is giving instructions to His disciples, before sending them out into the world. He says, "I am sending you out like sheep among wolves. Therefore be as shrewd as snakes and as innocent as doves." This is a strange word picture to me. How can someone be both shrewd and innocent? I can't imagine two more opposite creatures than snakes and doves. Yet Jesus calls them, and I believe us, to be both.

I think all of us, as parents, want to keep our children as innocent as doves. This is our natural inclination, but when our children are headed out into the world, Jesus also wants them to be "shrewd as snakes." Other translations of this verse use the words "wise" and "cunning" instead of shrewd. I think what Jesus is telling them is to keep their wits about them as they go out into the world. He wants them to use the intellect He gave them to keep a watchful eye on others and situations, while remaining true to themselves in response.

One reason I believe children need to develop the intellect God gave them is so they can be aware of their surroundings and to have the ability to reason through what they are told. The template against which all things are measured is, of course, the Scriptures, but our children need to know how to use the template and this takes the mind. Often the situation or the information our children receive is deceptive. This is where I want them to be shrewd. Shrewd enough to discern that something isn't quite right. Shrewd enough to reason out what that "something" is and make an appropriate response. I want them to be as wily as a snake and find a way to slither quickly past the danger. Being like a snake in danger will help keep them innocent like a dove.

Intellectual Maturity

Our children are on a journey to maturity — physical maturity, certainly, as well as spiritual maturity. They are also on a journey to develop their minds, to achieve an intellectual maturity. Paul puts it this way in 1 Corinthians 13:11: "When I was a child, I talked like a child, I thought like a child, I reasoned like a child. When I became a man, I put childish ways behind me." He goes on to say in Hebrews 5:4 that the mature have trained themselves by constant use to discern good from evil.

God's champions need a maturity that includes the ability to think and reason like an adult. Sadly, I have worked with many individuals in my practice who have never matured in their thinking and reasoning. This significantly hampers their ability to operate as a champion for God. They are constantly tripped up by this kind of faulty, immature reasoning. I have seen this over and over again in individuals who, for example, like children, believe that money will buy happiness. They reason, therefore, that if they can just get enough money, all of their problems will disappear. For years, under this faulty reasoning, they give up relationships, family, and even God in the pursuit of material wealth. They are simply too busy earning money to give much thought to what God wants them to do with their lives. Often, they end up with plenty of money and a lack of significant relationships. They have an oversized wallet and an undersized faith.

It's important for our children to develop to their fullest the intellect given to them by God. When they do so, they reach their intellectual maturity. Now, not every person has the same amount of intellect, but each person does have the amount needed to achieve the results God intends. Our job, as parents, is to assist our children in reaching that potential, no matter how much that is. We need to help them reach intellectual maturity. Remember, God expects us to love Him with all of our heart, our spirit, our bodies, and our minds. He gave us a brain and He has a purpose for it. He expects us to take His words and fix them in our minds, so they are accessible to us when we need them. He tells us to "Fix these words of mine in your hearts and minds; tie them as symbols on your hands and bind them on your foreheads" (Deut. 11:18).

Our children are responsible for their actions, but they are also responsible for their thoughts and the content of their minds. Psalm 7:9 and Jeremiah 17:10 tell us that God searches and examines the mind. Psalm 139:2 says that God perceives our thoughts "from afar." God wants us to achieve maturity in all aspects of our lives, so we are better able to serve Him and accomplish His purposes.

First Peter 1:13 tells us to "prepare your minds for action." This is my encouragement to you where your children are concerned — prepare the minds of your children for action:

- Don't neglect your child's intellectual development. Have a reason to reason.
- Make reasoning and intellectual discovery fun and exciting. Engage the mind by engaging the hands.
- Be involved in your child's education, whatever the setting. Be in charge of the ultimate curriculum, no matter who is the teacher.
- Help your child learn to reason from the Scriptures. Take a verse a week and see how many ways you can apply it to your life.
- Teach your child to be shrewd when it comes to the world. Help them put on their "God glasses" when they look at situations.
- Teach your child to be a lifelong learner of God. Help them to go and grow with God.

A Beautiful Mind

God considers your child to have a beautiful mind. It is the way He designed it, just for your child. As a parent, your job is to help your child realize his or her intellectual potential. But this intellectual potential must be groomed within the context of God's Word. When this is done, faith grows. Why, just look at the example of Abraham in the Old Testament. Abraham was called to use his mind everywhere God was concerned. After all, God kept giving him incredible assignments and kept giving him unbelievable promises. A lesser man would have rebelled, not understanding what God wanted. A lesser man might have obeyed, but without any real understanding of why. Not Abraham. Even when asked to do the unthinkable — murder his only son, Isaac — Abraham was using his intellect to figure things out. Hebrews 11:19, where Abraham's faith is commended, mentions this about his intellect: "Abraham reasoned that God could raise the dead, and figuratively speaking, he did receive Isaac back from death" (Heb. 11:19). Abraham *reasoned* and was able to put God's command to kill his son in context. Abraham reasoned and it reinforced his faith. Reason and faith are intimately connected. Do not buy into the world's lie that faith is only an unreasoned response to life. Teach your child that faith is a reasonable response to God.

Our children may be asked by God to do something equally as incomprehensible as Abraham. How can they obey if they have not learned to reason? Abraham's faith was remarkable and his faith was based, in part, on his ability to reason. Our children need to develop this same ability so their faith can be as strong as Abraham's. Then, they can say with confidence, "Test me, O LORD, and try me, examine my heart and my mind" (Ps. 26:2).

Our children's ability to reason, to know and understand God, to be able to put the world into context, is one of their greatest assets in life. Life will not always make sense. God will not always make sense. Faith will not always make sense. But if they can reason in the Lord, they will be able to say, like Jeremiah, "Yet this I call to mind and therefore I have hope" (Lam. 3:21). Our children need an arsenal of intellect to bolster their faith, so they can call truth to mind and refresh their hope.

Training Ground

There is no aspect of your life that is not a training ground for your child's intellectual development. We've already talked about how you can use the everyday events of your life to teach your child about God. Now, I'd like you to take it one step further. I'd like you to consider how you can use the everyday events of your life to provide an opportunity for your child to grow into the beautiful mind God intends.

Instead of telling your child about God, consider asking your child to tell you about God, through each particular circumstance. What does your child see as the lesson? Is your child able to think of a Scripture or biblical principle that applies to the situation?

I'd like you to think of three specific ways this week you can help your child's intellectual development. It might be taking a greater interest in your child's homework and what he or she is learning about in school. It could be asking your child questions about either a passage of Scripture you read or a prayer he or she says. It could be taking time to play a biblically based game and using this as a way to stimulate thought.

Much of what your child understands about God, about faith, and about Scripture will happen in the mind as a result of his or her private reasoning. Help your child's mind to develop depth of knowledge, discernment in application, and shrewdness in evaluation.

Teach your children to be aware of good and evil in the world. There are wolves and angels all around our children. Help them learn how to know the difference. Show them through your example how to live the difference by making wise, reasoned choices.

Father, You are the source of all knowledge and wisdom. You gave my child a mind, to use for You. Help me to be wise myself and know how to support my child's intellectual development. I want to be shrewd in using the circumstances and situations in my child's life to help develop a strong mind for You. I recognize that in order for me to assist my child in an intelligent faith, I need help to strengthen my own. Help me to know the mind of my child so I can join in the work of molding Your champion intellectually. My heart's desire is for my child to pray and sing and live life with spirit and with mind.

Chapter 9

Strong in
the Lord

*Finally, be strong in the Lord, and in the strength of his
might* (Eph. 6:10; NASB).

*Beloved, I pray that in all respects you may prosper and be in
good health, just as your soul prospers* (3 John 1:2; NASB).

I think all of us, as Christians, would agree there's a spiritual battle
going on over our children. God wants to bless them *every* way
and Satan wants to destroy them *any* way. Both God and Satan
have designs on our children and it behooves us to be aware of
both. As a Christian parent, it gives me great joy to recognize and
acknowledge God working in the lives of my children. As a father, it
just doesn't get much better than that! I need to ask myself, however,
if I am as alert to the ways Satan is trying to destroy my children.

Honestly, this is much harder for me to do. I'd much rather focus on the power of God in their lives than the influence of Satan. But as the adult, with greater spiritual maturity and insight — to say nothing of the lessons of personal experience, it's my job to be on the alert for the ways Satan seeks to destroy my children. They are young and vulnerable and it's one of my God-given duties, as a parent, to watch out for them. Is this a tremendous responsibility? Yes! Is this also a source of joy and purpose in my life? Absolutely!

Guardianship

At the Center, we serve many, many families. What rewarding work it is to bring families together for healing and reconciliation! It's what keeps all of us going in an often stressful, emotionally challenging profession. It is, after all, a ministry as well as a business, and we deal with many kinds of people and relationships. One of the relationships we work with is that of *guardian*. We deal with guardians who have been appointed to act in the best interests of either a child or, in some cases, an adult. We also deal with guardian-ad-litems, professionals who have been chosen by the court to guard the interests of an individual for a specific purpose. Often, it is to advocate for a child's interest in the midst of a divorce or custody proceeding. The more I think about this word and the relationship it describes, the more I realize I need to think of myself that way. I am a guardian.

Merriam-Webster's dictionary says that a guardian is someone who is a protector, a defender, a watcher. When Satan tries to destroy my children, I need to act as their guardian. I need to protect my child whenever possible, defend my child whenever necessary, and keep a constant watch for the forays of the enemy.

I certainly know God is a guardian and a watcher over my children. So, in this responsibility, I am not alone. However, it's still my job to watch over my children. We're in this guardianship together. I am an integral part of God's watch over my child. Listen to 2 Kings 11:5–7: "He commanded them, saying, 'This is the thing that you shall do: one third of you, who come in on the sabbath and keep watch over the king's house (one third also shall be at the gate Sur, and one third at the gate behind the guards), shall keep watch over the house for defense. And two parts of you, even all who go out on the sabbath, shall also keep watch over the house of the LORD for the king' " (NASB).

I love that passage for a couple of reasons. First, it's a partnership requiring teamwork. There is no lone watcher. In the same way, when I'm watching over my children, others are with me — my wife, my parents, our faith community. Each of us has a role to play, a watch to keep. Second, God has given me something infinitely more precious to watch over than a house — He's given me the temple that is my child. When I guard my children, I watch over temples of the Lord for my King. I have been entrusted with a watch to keep, and in that duty I need to be intentional and constant. Most of all, I need to guard my own behavior and choices to make sure I am not aiding and abetting the enemy.

The Land of Plenty

In this chapter, I want us to think about our duty as guardian over a specific aspect of our children — their physical bodies. These physical bodies, after all, are designed to house the very spirit of God. If Satan can attack them, can break down them physically, he can damage them spiritually. I've got to guard against this and daily pray John's prayer for my children: "Beloved, I pray that in all respects you may prosper and be in good health, just as your soul prospers" (3 John 1:2; NASB). My actions and decisions need to be made with my children's physical well-being in mind. Sometimes, this can appear to be a conflict of interest.

For my children to prosper physically, they need constant attention. I'm a fairly busy guy, with lots of demands all clamoring for my attention. As I try to fit fatherhood into that active schedule, I must remember my children's physical bodies need plenty of nutrition, plenty of water, plenty of exercise, and plenty of rest. If I fail to pay attention to these details over a long enough period of time, the health of my children suffers and Satan is presented a golden opportunity to subvert a pint-sized temple of the living God.

Children are amazingly resilient but they are also fragile. I can go all day on a few cups of coffee, a gallon of water, and a nutrition bar. This isn't something I plan, but there have been days when that's about all I get until I'm home at night. My children, on the other hand, need to eat. If they don't, they get tired, cranky, and depleted. Their bodies are growing and absolutely demand the nutrients, hydration, exercise, and rest necessary to do so. While I may deprive myself of a good night's sleep or work through lunch in order to catch up, I wouldn't dream of asking this of my children. In this, I'm probably pretty much like you. We're good parents. What troubles me, though, is how easy it is to veer off course.

Jesus, in Luke 11, tells a story about parenting. He uses an example of an earthly father to help his audience understand about their heavenly one. It goes like this: "Now suppose one of you fathers is asked by his son for a fish; he will not give him a snake instead of a fish, will he? Or if he is asked for an egg, he will not give him a scorpion, will he? If you then, being evil, know how to give good gifts to your children, how much more shall your heavenly Father give the Holy Spirit to those who ask Him?" (Luke 11:11–13; NASB). This parable illustrates a powerful point about God's goodness. It also shows that even we know how to be good parents.

We know how to be good parents but we don't always choose to put that knowledge into action. Over the course of my work, I've seen parents who actually did give their child a snake instead of a fish and a scorpion instead of an egg. Oh, not literally, of course, but figuratively. When the child wanted no part of either the snake or the scorpion, chaos ensued and the family ended up at the Center. Parents come in to the Center, beside themselves over the behavior of their children. These children are basically out of control — hyper, defiant, aggressive. After meeting with us for a while, I can understand why. These children are reacting from always being given snakes and scorpions. I'd be a little wild, too! When we explain to the parents that their children are merely reacting to what they're being given, it makes all the difference in the world. We help parents to see the snakes and scorpions for what they are.

As I said, children need plenty of nutrition; instead these children are given plenty of fast food. Instead of plenty of water, they are given plenty of soda. Instead of plenty of exercise, they are given plenty of television, computer time, and video games. Instead of plenty of rest, they are given plenty of stress. When put this way, the negatives are easier to see and the negative behavior easier to understand.

What happens when parents give their children something harmful but don't see it as such? Children react to the harm and go wild. The parent misinterprets the child's reaction and wants the behavior changed. I don't call this misbehavior, I call it inevitable. I call it a natural consequence. If your child is bitten by a snake or a scorpion, your child will react. If you fill your child up with junk food and pop, sit them in front of an electronic device for hours a day, and create a hectic, stressful home environment, your child will also react. We help parents to see the snakes and scorpions they are giving their children for what they are — harmful. This isn't about blame, but about education. Once parents are educated to the damage being done to the bodies of their children by the choices they make, changes can occur. Again, children are resilient and their growing bodies respond to healthy eating, lots of physical activity, and time for rest and sleep. Over and over again, as we've worked with families, we see the positive effect on behavior these physical changes bring about. It's common sense, really. Works the same for us, as adults, doesn't it? If I eat nutritious food, drink plenty of water, get out and get moving, and make sure to rest well at night, I feel better. I think better. I act better. When I feel, think, and act better, it's harder for Satan to get to me. I'm stronger, less vulnerable.

Believe me, I'm well aware of what happens when I'm tired, cranky, and depleted myself. I can't seem to concentrate. Small hurdles seem like huge obstacles. I have the patience of a gnat. When presented with a feel-good alternative, I take it, regardless of the consequences. And I'm just trying to get through the day, not accomplish the physical transformation from child to adult.

In a land of plenty, as far as food is concerned, it's hard to believe there is so much miss-nutrition. It's not really malnutrition but miss-nutrition; we miss the mark where nutrition is concerned, not because of lack of good food but because of lack of good choices.

For our children to grow strong in the Lord, they need to be physically fit. He's got things for them to do that require their physical bodies.

Strong and Courageous

From the beginning of time, God has given people physical tasks to do. Before the Fall, our job was to tend the garden. Now, for those of you who work around your yards, you know what physical work this is! After the Fall, God still had in mind for us to work the land, only now it was going to be a lot harder. Over most of the course of human history, our lives have consisted of physical activity. When God chose a people for himself, He physically moved them about from one land to the next, over long distances. They were required to walk and move to accomplish God's will.

Repeatedly in the Old Testament, the people of Israel are told to be "strong and courageous." Do I believe we are to be spiritually strong? Yes, but I believe this admonition is also to be physically strong. After all, these people weren't merely on a hike, they were living in the wilderness, actively engaged in battle to win the land the Lord had given them. This was a warrior people, whose very lives were to conquer for God. They were champions and they needed their physical strength to carry out God's will in their lives.

Our children may not be literally fighting battles or living in the wilderness, but the tasks God has in mind for them will still be carried out in their physical bodies. We need to help prepare them emotionally, intellectually, spiritually, and physically to be ready for whatever God calls them to do. If they are unhealthy or physically out of shape, this will be a hindrance. As we join God in this work to mold His champion, we need to remember not to neglect the physical health of our children.

For more information on this topic, see my book *Healthy Habits, Happy Kids* listed in the resource section of this chapter.

Choice Food

Let's talk for a minute about the choices we can make when feeding our children. In this day and age, there are a lot of them! Just walk into the average grocery store and take a walk down the cereal aisle. This is just one type of food for one meal of the day. There are boxes after boxes of different types and flavors. If you were to investigate each type of cereal, you'd be there for hours. Most of us don't have that kind of time. So, what do we do? We ask our kids, "What kind of cereal do you want?" It seems a simple enough question. The problem is, we often take their answer, grab it and go. We've basically passed the ball of choice into the court of our kids — and they've got some interesting players on their sidelines.

Have you watched the commercials on television lately, especially during children's programming? Advertisers are not interested in the health of your children. They are interested in selling their products to your children, whether those products are good for them or not. Our children are inundated with pressure from these powerful messages to choose calorie-rich, nutrient-poor foods. Foods full of fat, sugar, and salt, produced to look and taste great. The packaging is bright and cartoonish, with recognizable characters. A great deal of research is devoted to attracting children to this type of food. When you ask your child, "What kind of cereal do you want?" nutritional content is not a factor for a five year old.

Okay, this example may be a bit over the top for some of you, but it represents the type of choices we, as parents, make all the time with our kids. We're busy, tired, and stressed ourselves and so we're willing to let our kids make the choices so we don't have to fight one more battle before we can finally get home and take our shoes off. Maybe we've worked longer than we should and we feel guilty so we take our kids for fast food instead of cooking a meal at home. It just seems easier to give in, to make them happy. The problem is, what makes them happy for the moment doesn't always make them healthy for the long term.

Giving in to our kids once or twice is not a problem. When they dictate what they eat over and over again, it is. Children do not understand about nutrition and the role it plays in their physical development. If left to their own devices, many would choose to eat sweets and fats all the time. How do I know? Because I work with adults who grow up, make those same choices now that they can, and end up overweight, ill, and unhappy.

The growing body is an intricate organism, designed by God to transform a person from an infant into an adult. This not only takes a great deal of time and energy, it takes a great deal of nutrition. A young body is under construction and requires materials and resources to complete assembly. Children are the best judge of when they are hungry, but they are not the best judge of what to eat when hungry. They need guidance and oversight. When the adults around them make good food choices, children learn what is good to eat and why. In this day and age, it's not an easy lesson.

We don't eat the same way we used to. Our portions are bigger. Our food is fatter and sweeter. Basic nutrients have been processed out for the sake of convenience. Health-life considerations have given way to shelf-life considerations. Much of the food processed today may look and taste better, but it certainly isn't better for you.

It may seem like an impossible task to help your kids eat healthier, but it doesn't have to be. Here are few simple suggestions to help you get back on the right track where the nutrition of your kids is concerned.

1. *Eat healthier yourself.* Your child is an imitator; what you do, he or she will want to do. It doesn't help to put broccoli on your child's plate while you're eating cookies. Your child will instantly perceive this to be an injustice and complain loudly! And why not? You serve your child by the example you set. Serve your child well by eating well yourself. (Look at the last chapter for information about my book *The Total Temple Makeover*. Let your desire to improve the health of your child motivate you to make changes for yourself.)

2. *Eat whole foods.* Avoid as many processed foods as you can. Processed, packaged foods often strip out nutrients and put in extra fats, sugars, and salts. God made our bodies to respond to good food. It may take a while for the palate to change, but it can be done. Have patience and don't give up on the nutrition of your family!

3. *Eat fresh fruits and vegetables.* These are about as "whole" as you can get. Just wash, cut them up into bite-sized pieces, and you're ready to go. For portability, place in a sealable plastic bag.

4. *Eat whole grains.* Look for breads, pastas, and flour made of whole grains. These have a higher nutritional value and more dietary fiber.

5. *Eat a variety.* Kids tend to have one thing they like and want to eat it all the time. Help your child learn variety by providing different types of flavors and textures in food. We call them "food potions." The kitchen is a place where we explore, enjoy, and play with food. My children learn that it isn't just the taste that's important with food but the preparation and the fellowship. It's about the potions not the portions!

6. *Eat lean meats and fish.* Growing bodies need protein! Look for leaner cuts of meat to avoid the animal fats. Choose fish several times a week. It's naturally lean and many kinds have beneficial Omega-rich essentially fatty acids. If you've got a child who doesn't really like fish, we've got a great product we sell at the Center called *Coromega*. It's an omega product that comes in something like a small catsup package and tastes like orange. Kids think it tastes great; they don't realize how good it is for them.

7. *Avoid an abundance of fried foods.* Frying adds fat to food. Instead, eat food raw, baked, grilled, sautéed, or roasted.

8. *Watch for trans-fats.* Many of the trans-fats we eat today come from the hydrogenated oils used in crackers, cookies, and cakes. The molecular structure of the fat is altered so it holds together longer and increases the shelf-life of food. This change in molecular structure has the nasty side effect of clogging up our arteries over time.

8. *Limit processed sweets.* There's nothing wrong with a cookie after dinner, but one shouldn't turn into five or six. Instead, make it a cookie and a serving of yogurt or piece of fruit.

9. *Use the 30-30-40 rule.* Watch food labels and strive for 40% of your child's calories to be from complex carbohydrates, 30% from protein and 30% from fats.

10. *Choose your fats.* Look for unsaturated fats, high in Omega 3 and 6. These fats are found in nuts, flax seed, fish, and olive oil. Fats are an important nutrient for the body. They aid lubrication and brain function. Don't fall into the trap of thinking all fat is bad. It's not, and your child needs the right kinds of fats to grow a championship body.

11. *Give your child a good multi-vitamin, multi-mineral each day.* Even with healthy eating, it's difficult to get all of the trace minerals and vitamins needed to operate optimally. Each vitamin, each mineral, each amino acid, acts as a piece of the nutritional puzzle. For the puzzle to be complete, all the pieces need to be there. Today, there are many good products available, even for children. Look for a multi-formula designed for the age of your children (for older children, often they will have the label of "junior"). Choose a product that has high bio-availability — a formula that your child's digestive system can actually break down and use, with organically based ingredients.

Plumping on Pop

Childhood obesity is on the rise, caused by a variety of societal factors. One of the most surprising to me, when I first read it, was the rise in consumption of soft drinks among children. Pop is plumping our kids. Soda represents hundreds of empty calories, which add on the pounds day after day. Our children now drink more soda than they do milk or water. Too much rots their teeth and expands their waistlines.

I'm trying to remember when all this pop drinking started. Frankly, we just didn't have a lot of pop around our house growing up. We had milk or water; that was it for most of the week. On Sundays, before church, we could have Dr. Pepper when we went to our grandparents. I guess growing up I viewed soda almost like a dessert. It was special, a treat, not something you had every day. Today, it is neither special nor a treat, and our kids have a lot of it every day.

True, there are plethora of diet sodas available, but I do not recommend these for children. They contain a swill of artificial ingredients and manufactured sweeteners. There isn't any reason why children should be drinking these.

Okay, so what should children drink? Water, and lots of it. Milk, every day, (unless lactose intolerant and then there are several excellent soy substitutes) and some fruit juice. Put another way — more water than milk, more milk than juice. What do I have against fruit juice? Well, it contains a great deal of sugar. I'd much rather a child had an orange than a glass of orange juice, or an apple instead of a glass of apple juice. Not only do they get the nutrients of the whole fruit, they get the fiber.

Food for the Stomach

Before we get to the other components of good health for your children — exercise and rest — I want to leave just one more thought about eating healthy. You want your child to understand about food and nutrition and make good choices. You do not, however, want your child to become obsessed with food. This is about health and nutrition, about the wonderful workings of the body and God's grand design. It is not about fear of fat or treating the body as an enemy. Children need to be educated about health, not conditioned to fear. In my line of work, I've seen the damage done by parents — often mothers — who transfer their fear of food and fat to their children.

One of the main issues we work with at the Center is eating disorders. This could range from a 13-year-old boy who refuses to eat, to a 50-year-old woman whose obesity is the result of years of stuffing her pain, to a 24-year-old woman who vomits up the food she's eaten for fear of being fat. From anorexia to bulimia to compulsive binge or overeating, each eating disorder does tremendous damage to the person physically and consumes their thoughts, energy, time, and very life. When I see this happen, I see Satan at work. I see beautiful, vibrant children of God, champions of God, derailed by their obsession with food and weight. Any thought of what they might do for God is subjugated to their singular preoccupation with food. For them, food takes on a significance in their lives it was never meant to fill. Food is not a means to happiness, fulfillment, satisfaction, or comfort. It is the nutritional fuel we need to power this miraculous gift from God, our bodies. For happiness, fulfillment, satisfaction, and comfort, God has other avenues. Can a good meal be satisfying? Sure, but it's a problem when the only source of these feelings is food.

Universally, those we see with an eating disorder hate their bodies. They find them fat, ugly, unlovable. Because they hate their bodies, they abuse their bodies. When they abuse their bodies, they damage the temple of God and grieve the Holy Spirit. We want our children to learn to eat healthy so they can learn to love their bodies. Loving our bodies should be a given. In fact, it is a given, as far as Scripture is concerned. Ephesians 5:29 says, "For no one ever hated his own flesh, but nourishes and cherishes it, just as Christ also does the church" (NASB). God intends for each one of us to love our bodies, to nourish and cherish them. Eating healthy is one way to do this. I do not want any more of our children to grow up hating their bodies; I know the tragedy this causes. I want each of them to love their bodies, to consider their body to be the body of God's champion.

God designed eating and drinking to be pleasurable, but just like all things pleasurable, He wants us to exercise good judgment. This is a gift we can pass on to our children, through our example, our words, and our lives. If this is an area of challenge for you, I urge you to seek assistance from a healthcare professional. If you have difficulty with food and weight issues, these will be observed by your children and will affect their relationship to their own bodies, food, and weight. Not only will you be healthier, so will your children. It's really a win-win situation! (If you are concerned about your child and an eating disorder, or yourself and an eating disorder, you can go online to the Center's website at www.aplaceofhope.com. There, you'll find a confidential eating disorder survey you can take. It is meant for adults and older teens. After you submit your survey, you'll receive back an appropriate response, given your score. In addition, there is a great deal about eating disorders on the Center's website and on our other website, www.caringonline.com. If you're worried, get more information. You can also call us at (888) 771-5166 to ask questions and get answers.)

Ready, Set, Go!

We've talked about healthy eating and proper hydration for our children. Health isn't just about what you take into your body it's also about what you do with your body. Our children were meant to be physical. They were meant to run, jump, skip, bike, skate. They were meant to spend time outdoors, in the air, in the sun, playing and moving. This used to be synonymous with childhood. Not anymore.

As the world of children has shrunk, the bodies of children have grown. Parents, fearful of the dangers of modern society, are afraid to let their children out-of-doors and out-of-sight. Latch-key children come home from school and barricade themselves inside the family fortress, waiting for a parent to come home and free them. To keep them company in this compound is often a television, a computer, a video game, and a pantry full of snacks. Their mind is occupied while their muscles atrophy. How sad this is!

I understand that most families today are made up of two incomes. Both my wife, LaFon, and I work, but we make it a priority for one of us to be available to our children in the late afternoon and early evening during the week. We go to the park, participate in organized sports, throw the ball at home, go walking on the beach. We find a way for our children to get out and get moving every day. On the weekends, there is a great deal we could do with that time as working parents, but what we do is play with Gregg and Benjamin. We do "explore walks" where we head outside for no other reason than to just see what we see.

If your children are grade school aged, it's not enough to expect the physical play at school to be enough. If you've followed the debate about educational standards and testing, you are probably already aware of how schools are trading in physical education for academic catch-up. This is so short-sided. All children need to move and play, as a way to refresh themselves and enhance the learning experience. All work and no play really does make Jack a dull boy! It's not that great for Jane, either. Don't count on whatever recess time your child gets at school to fulfill all of their exercise needs. You need to be prepared to provide your child with more.

Do you remember one of the best ways the Bible says you can teach your children? It was "walking down the road." Walking is good for teaching and it's good for exercise. One way you can help your child get out of the house and get more exercise is to go along. Take a walk, have a talk. My children are young and this is one of the best ways for us to spend time together. I realize as they get older, and more involved in organized sports, these walk-talks will diminish. I'm determined, however, to continue to make them a part of our lives as often as I can, for as long as I can.

I've already talked about taking Gregg to the park. Sometimes I just take one of the boys, sometimes both. My goal is to get outside with my kids, enjoy the day, relax, and have fun. Physical play is fun and should be. I'm not pushing Gregg to join the major leagues when we play ball or training Benjamin to run a four-minute mile when we run down a hill. There is no pressure here to perform, just get out and have fun. We race across the grass, not to win, but because it feels good to run. There will be time enough as they get older to introduce the concept of competition and for them to understand the wisdom of exercise. For now, I just want my children to associate physical activity with enjoyment.

How much physical activity is your child getting each day? If this isn't an issue for you, congratulations! Many of us, however, face a challenge in making sure our kids are getting enough. I encourage you to establish a habit of spending time, as often as you can, being physically active with your children. Do something, even if it's just a walk around the neighborhood with the dog.

Try a variety of activities. If one doesn't seem to "gel" with your child, try another. Your child needs to develop the habit of exercise. After all, we're not fighting physical battles or walking miles a day anymore. We're sitting in cars, sitting at work, sitting at home. For most of us, our lives are sedentary and we must exercise daily to make up for it. I cannot imagine it will be vastly different for our own kids. With technology continuing to provide "convenience" in our lives, it takes less and less physically to do our jobs. To keep our bodies operating physically, we need to exercise. This is our reality and it's the reality for our kids. Help your children find a physical activity they enjoy and help build a habit, a routine, a lifestyle, that includes this physical activity. They will thank you now, for the fun it is, and they'll thank you later, for the example it is.

Restoration

Sometimes, in the midst of my busy life, I forget to rest. I somehow think that I'll be able to do more if I keep going and cheat sleep. I'll go through a period of time where I'll get to bed too late and get up in the morning too early. Generally, it's because I think I have too much to do and I think this schedule will help me. I'm not sure why I keep buying this lie, but I do, even though it doesn't work! When I'm tired, it takes me longer to do just about everything. I make more mistakes. I can't think clearly. I start taking short cuts and compromise the quality of the job. In the end, I'm working harder and longer and accomplishing less. What I really need to do is put it down, clear my mind, relax my body, and go to sleep. Then, when I wake up refreshed, I'm able to accomplish what I need in the time I have.

This go-go-go cycle isn't good for me; I know this. It isn't good for anyone, especially our children. When we suck our children into our hectic, frantic, break-neck paced lives, we rob them of their childhood. We teach them about the stress involved in being an adult before they've even had the opportunity to be kids. Once again, they're asking for an egg and we give them a scorpion; they just want time to enjoy their childhood and we've chained them to our adult-sized schedules. Our children are not just "along for the ride" where our daily schedules are concerned. They are people, in their own right, with their own schedules and needs. What they need is time to be kids. They need time to grow and play, and they need time to rest.

God, the Creator of the universe, the crafter of our champion, took time to rest. He's fairly important and moderately busy. In the midst of creating the universe and everything in it, He took time to reflect on and rest from what He'd done. If it's appropriate for God, it's appropriate for His champion. God rested, so I need to rest and my child needs to rest.

Notice, I didn't say *sleep*. To me, there's a difference. To me, resting is about letting go and easing into that blessed state of relaxation, where your body and your mind wind down from the day. Once you're in a restful state, you're able to go to sleep. Rest prepares you for sleep. If we're not careful, we schedule sleep as rigidly as we do the rest of our day. We determine that at precisely 10:05 p.m., we must be asleep so we can get up at 5:27 a.m. to start our day. We compound the problem by working like crazy right up to 10:04 p.m. and expect that miraculously our bodies will cooperate and go to sleep on command. I don't know about you, but this really doesn't work too well for me. To get a really good night's sleep, I need to rest and prepare first.

Our children are no different. They need transition time. They must be prepared for sleep. If they are not, bedtime turns into a battle royale, with a geared-up, stressed-out child refusing to sleep on command. Often, the difficulties children have with bedtime is not over bed, it's over time — their time with you. Bedtime can seem like an abrupt abandonment of their connection with their parents. If a child feels neglected, stressed, unsettled before going to bed, he or she is not going to surrender easily. In order to get even a few minutes more with you, they're willing to pitch a fit in order to capture your attention. They need your attention and they'll do what it takes to get it, even if it means yelling, crying, and disobeying. It's negative attention from you, but it is still attention. Unless a child has a calm, connected closure with you at the end of the day, it could turn out to be a long night. If this has just described your house at night, you're not alone. Nighttime battles are not uncommon. Take heart, however, because this is a battle you and your child can win together. Here are a few suggestions I've found to be very effective in preparing your child for sleep.

Make bedtime a routine. Keep things at the same time and in the same order, as much as possible. Children feel secure when they know what to expect.

Be consistent with your routine. If you allow too many exceptions, the exceptions will become the rule and you're back to square one.

Allow enough time for your bedtime routine. Children are not electronic appliances; you cannot just flip a switch and expect them to turn off. Be realistic about how much time it takes to go through your routine. Remember, this is a calm and restful preparation time for sleep. If you're jamming to rush through your routine, so you can mark off all the boxes, you've just turned bedtime into every other part of your hectic day. Believe me, your child will feel your stress and respond accordingly.

Include restful activities in the bedtime routine. A nice hot bath for younger children or shower for older children is physically relaxing. Snuggling up with a good book before bed, when your child is warm after a bath and clothed in comfortable jammies is physically relaxing. Think low-key, think personally connecting. Avoid electronic interaction. No television, computers, or video games. These can hype your child up instead of calm your child down. What your child needs is time with you, time to connect, be reminded of how much you love them and how important they are to you. Surrounded by this love and assurance, your child can relax and prepare for sleep.

Take time to pray and read the Bible with your children at night. As your child is immersed in the love you have for him or her, it's a great time to remind them of the love of God. When you talk about God as their father, your love as a parent is immediate and impressive. They will understand about God through you.

Limit stimuli. Turn down the lights in the house. Turn off the television or radio. The entire house should enter a "quiet zone" at bedtime. If the rest of the house is "jumping" with activity, your child may well feel left out and abandoned at bedtime. The "important" people get to stay up; bedtime becomes a punishment. When you set the stage for rest in the whole house, your child is participating in a family ritual. They're included, they're not left out. It makes the separation of sleep easier.

Why all this attention on sleep and the rest it takes to achieve it? Your child must have ample sleep to grow up strong and healthy. Sleep is the time for your child's body to repair and to grow. Sleep is not a static time for growing children; it is an active time for the body. Have you ever heard parents who remark that it seems their child has "grown overnight"? There's something to that!

Children need more sleep than adults. Do not make the mistake of so enmeshing your child's schedule into yours that you extend this into the amount of sleep your child receives. Your child needs more, all the way through adolescence. Robbing your child of sleep has serious physical consequences. Lack of sleep puts the body into stress-mode and catapults children into adult-onset type conditions: hypertension, obesity, heart disease. Sadly, these used to be the sole realm of adulthood, but are creeping slowly and slowly younger, as children begin to mirror adult conditions. Let your children be children for as long as they can! Treat them as children; treat childhood as precious and valuable and worth preserving for as long as you can.

Training Ground

We've seen previously from 1 Corinthians 6:19 that the bodies of our children were created to be a temple of the Holy Spirit. Your child's body is kind of on loan to you by God. He wants to mold their hearts, their minds, their spirits, and their bodies into a whole-person champion for Him. Frankly, He's got plans for them, things He wants them to accomplish and experience. Each child is given a body, created by God, through which these plans are to be carried out. In fact, your child's body doesn't belong to him or her. It also doesn't belong to you. You're a guardian over the body of your child and it's time to take stock of how that guardianship is going.

I want you to take a piece of paper (or do this in your mind if you're absolutely against any sort of artistic endeavor at your age — though I encourage you to do this anyway!) and draw a large square in the center of the paper. Draw a different box for each of your children. You have just created a walled city, with your child in the middle.

Next, put your name on each of the corners of the square. You are the watcher, the guardian, of this walled city.

Now, place outside the walls all of the physical challenges your child faces. Where is Satan working to attack your child's body?

Meditate on your child's life, what you know about your child, and what happens to him or her each day. How much physical activity is there? How much stress? Is your child eating and drinking in a healthy manner? Does your child take a nutritional supplement?

Draw a line in the middle of the page, underneath the square. On the left side, take each challenge and elaborate. On the right side, formulate a defense strategy. How will you defend your child against this attack? What additional reinforcements do you need to gather to assist in the defense? How are you going to enlist the aid of these reinforcements?

This is just a graphic representation of what's happening with your child physically right now. It's also an excellent exercise to use for other aspects of your child's life, not merely his or her physical well-being. Take time to stop and reflect on what is happening with your child right now. Then, act. Face the challenges and come up with a strategy to change your child's life for good, today.

Now, pray over your city. Remember, you are a watcher for this temple of the Lord for your King.

Of all the gifts You've given me, Lord, I thank You for the gift of being a watcher over my child. I know this child belongs to You and I thank You for the opportunity to love, raise, and care for this precious soul. Help me to be honest about how I am guarding my child's physical health. I confess I often take short cuts that benefit me but harm my child. I need the strength to stop and put my child first. Help me to make the positive changes I need, in order to benefit my child. Especially when it means I must change my own health habits. Give me the motivation and the strength to do what's right for myself, so I can do what's right for my child.

Support

God created us as individuals. He loves us as individuals. He knows us as individuals. Christ died for us as individuals. In order for me to support the budding champion that is my child, I need to approach him or her as an individual — unique in God's eyes. My sons, Gregg and Benjamin, are very different people. What works with one doesn't automatically work with the other. I have to approach them as individuals, not only in teaching or discipline, but also in how I show and provide support. Support is only effective if it is tailored to the child. After all, it doesn't help to put a gold fish in the ocean or a tuna in a river. Both are fish, but they need different types of environments to support them. God knows this about fish; I need to know this about my child.

> *Listen from your home in heaven, forgive and reward us: reward each life and circumstance, for you know each life from the inside (you're the only one with such inside knowledge!), so they'll live before you in lifelong reverence and believing obedience on this land you gave our ancestors* (2 Chron. 6:30–31; TM).

Chapter 10

Support for Girls

Charm is deceptive, and beauty is fleeting; but a woman who fears the LORD is to be praised. Give her the reward she has earned, and let her works bring her praise at the city gate (Prov. 31:30–31).

I am generally in awe of my wife. She's an amazing person with an abundance of gifts and talents. She loves the Lord with all her heart and reminds me daily of what it means to be a servant of God. I guess I've loved her strength of character from the moment I met her in college. When I met LaFon, she was really a sort of orphan. Her father had died a year earlier; her mother had already passed away and gone from her life. She could have been bitter about losing both parents so young, but she wasn't. As I got to know her, she told me she always felt protected by God because of her faith. She accepted the circumstances of her life and chose to trust God. Even with so much tragedy in her life, she excelled in school and was named marketing student of the year in the business school. Though missing significant relationships in her life, she did not choose short cuts to intimacy but preserved herself in all regards. I've never met someone so courageous, so humble, so much a champion of God. An incredible woman of God — and a champion of God. She is not alone; she has many sisters.

I am around women every day: LaFon, the women who work with me at the Center, those girls and women who come to us for help. I've seen women in just about every circumstance in life. I've heard their stories and seen their hearts. Women are often the prime motivator in reaching out for help in a challenging family situation. Because of this, I have the utmost respect for women. Sometimes, though, I think God gave me sons to help balance out my life. I am a male in a sea of females.

Now, it may seem that having only sons puts me at a disadvantage to speak about daughters. I may not have learned lessons from daughters of my own, but over the past 20-plus years, I've learned a great deal from yours. I've seen them at all ages, from little girl to mature woman. From sharing their pain and difficulties, their triumphs and victories in life, I've developed a deep admiration. Your daughters have taught me what's important to them, what gives them great joy and what causes them immeasurable pain. So, what I'm going to share in this chapter comes from them, as well as from me.

The Female Champion

What do you think of when you hear the term "warrior princess"? Several years ago, there was a television show called "Xena" which featured a tall, strong, leather-clad female who could fight even better than men. She went about the countryside in some far off, mythical land, battling for justice and the triumph of good over evil. This may be what comes to your mind when you think of a female champion — someone who is able to remain a woman while besting men in every area of life. As entertaining as that show may have been to many, it wasn't just mythical in location. It perpetuated the myth that for a woman to be a champion she needed to enter a man's arena and win.

Whoever said a woman needed to be like a man to be a true champion? Whoever said it obviously felt that true champions are male. This is not God's view. His champions come in both genders and have similar and unique features. If brute strength was all it took to be a whole champion of God, Samson would have fit the bill. Instead, as we've learned, he was woefully inadequate.

Expecting women to be men in order to be champions makes for a decidedly unlevel playing field. Granted, there are some women who will be stronger than some men, but the sheer fact of our gender-based physiology dictates that men will — in general — be stronger than women. It has to do with the distribution of hormones between genders. Men have higher levels of testosterone, which promotes lean muscle development. Women have higher levels of estrogen, which promotes a greater percentage of body fat. Healthy women have a higher body fat percentage than healthy men. In so many ways, women are not men and men are not women. We are different.

Thirty years ago, saying that men and women were different in anything but reproductive physiology was considered cultural heresy. Emerging from a chauvinistic era where females were considered less than males, we were told there was no significant difference between males and females and that any difference there was came about through socialization and not innate nature. The male and female brains, we were told, are no different. When girls and boys acted differently, it was because they were taught to act differently and not because they were following some pre-ordained pattern.

For Christians, this world view created a problem, for we believe that God made us male and female, separate and distinct, in His plan. We kept advocating for nature versus nurture where genders were concerned. This view was considered parochial and patriarchal, meant to keep females subjugated within the confines of antiquated, repressive religious beliefs. Undaunted, Christians continued to point out the ways little boys acted like, well, boys, and little girls acted like girls, even from birth. For years, this view kept Christians pretty much out in the cold as feminism took center stage in American cultural thought.

It did something else very destructive, as well, I believe. It taught little girls that there was something wrong in wanting to be feminine. If a woman wanted to choose maintaining a home instead of a career, she was betraying her sex. If a woman wanted to have children instead of a higher education, she was intellectually stunted. Because society did not recognize the differences in men and women, they ridiculed those who made decisions based upon those differences. In attempting to open up more doors to women in society, they keep closing traditional doors of family, femininity, and mothering. They told women what they should and should not view as important, whether the individual woman agreed or not. This attitude was not, at its core, liberating.

Women are natural nurturers. They are intensely, sometimes painfully, aware of the web of relationships in which they move. When those webs are tattered, women feel it and respond. It is no accident that women represent the majority of people we see at the Center. Is it because women are somehow more fragile emotionally than men? No; it's because women often are the ones who choose to fight for their spouse, their children, their lives, their recovery. In my view, these women are champions. They alone have the courage to enter the arena of relationships and fight for what they value.

Champion of Connections

A friend of mine took his young daughter fishing with him. As he recalls, she was probably around nine, old enough to pay attention to his instructions, enjoy the beauty of the outdoors, and hold a pole in the water. She fished with him for a while and then, as children often do, became bored with the waiting, choosing instead to explore the rocks and pools along the riverbank. Her job was to hold the net ready, in case he caught a fish.

Before long, he had a fish on the line. Reeling it in, he instructed her to place the net underneath the fish and bring it up to the surface so he could remove the hook. It was a bright, plump steelhead (an ocean-going trout), big enough to keep. Looking at it, all my friend could think about was how good it was going to taste, marinated and smoked!

His daughter, however, saw something quite different when she looked at the fish. Realizing he meant to keep it, she stood up to him, as furious and indignant as only a nine-year-old girl can be.

"Daddy!" she cried, "you can't keep him! You have to let him go!"

"Why?" he asked, perplexed at her response, sure he'd explained the goal of fishing in the car on the way to the river.

"Because," she replied with conviction, "he has a family! You can't take him away from his family. You have to put him back!" Her attitude was incredulous; she expected nothing else from her father than to do the right thing, as she saw it.

Taking a deep breath, he gently lowered the steelhead back into the water, where it swished its tail and slid back into the current.

"Thank you, Daddy," his little girl said, hugging him tightly. At that moment, he realized the definition of hero could be vastly different for a daughter than for a son.

Our daughters are champions of connections. They have a God-given ability to understand how things and people fit together. Some people call it being relational. At that moment while fishing, my friend was tempted to call it irrational. But, in that millisecond between confrontation and decision, he recognized something profound about his daughter — she saw the world in terms of how one thing fit in with another, in terms of relationships. Naturally, she wouldn't even consider keeping the fish if it meant it would be separated from its family, its connection. In the eyes of a nine-year-old girl, that connection was worth protecting. His daughter stood up to him, in order to champion the concept of connections, of relationships.

Author and researcher Michael Gurian calls this the intimacy imperative, in his ground-breaking book *The Wonder of Girls* (Atria Books, 2002). He persuasively speaks about this desire to connect through relationships as being "nature-based." Through his research into female physiology, brain structure, and development, Gurian believes it is in the nature of girls to value and seek out these "webbed mysteries of intimate connections in nearly all their interactions (p. 55)." Now, reading Gurian's book is a little bit like eating fish; enjoy the meat but pick out the bones. Gurian credits a girl's behavior to her innate "nature"; I credit her innate nature to God.

From the beginning, God made woman to exist within relationships. She was made to exist in relationship to man. Through her relationship with man, she was made to exist within relationship to family. In Genesis 3:20, "Adam named his wife Eve, because she would become the mother of all the living." Women are attuned to relationship, to connection, being designed by God for this very important function.

It should not surprise us, then, when even our young daughters place great importance in family. Little girls will mimic family when playing with dolls and stuffed animals. A little girl will cuddle a baby doll. A little boy will point it like a weapon. This is not exclusively nurture; it is decidedly nature, her God-given nature.

It is not realistic, then, to expect our champion daughters to choose the same arenas as our sons. It is not realistic, then, to expect our champion daughters to choose the same methods of conquest as our sons. They are different, with different natures and different motivations in the world. If we expect our daughters to act like sons, we devalue them as daughters.

At the Center, we treat adolescent girls, many of whom are struggling with an eating disorder. Each girl's story is unique, as they bring individual pain to a collective disorder. Several of the young girls we've treated began their slide to anorexia in a desire to avoid puberty. To them, starving in order to retard their growing body's imperative to develop breasts, hips, and begin menses, was worth the struggle. Several have hated their emerging sexuality because, in their minds, it meant a loss of connection with their father, a father who wanted a son more than a daughter, a father who valued a son more than a daughter. The desire for connection, for value and worth within the relationship, was so strong it was worth the risk of death.

We must recognize that God designed our daughters. If He designed them, then we must trust they are well designed for the arenas He has in mind for them to champion. Does He mean for them to stand up and defend the family? I believe this is so with all my heart. Those who understand the problem are given the responsibility to seek the solution. Women often see the problem in the family and are empowered by God to stand up and champion the family.

Granted, not all of our daughters will have families, but this does not alter their basic nature. Women without children often champion the causes of the weak and powerless, acting as "global mothers," tirelessly advocating for change, for redress, for justice. Michael Gurian, in *The Wonder of Girls,* ascribes these traits to the neurological and physiological female development of the moral and spiritual aspects of the human brain. He argues that females develop these areas of the brain in greater degree and at an earlier age than males. (While certainly not written from a Christian point of view, Gurian's book uses the latest in brain and body research to highlight the physical differences between females and males. I encourage everyone to read this book, filtering his examples and conclusions through the wisdom of Scripture. More often than not, I found myself nodding my head in agreement.)

Champion of Cleaving

Any of you readers who have teenage or even pre-teen daughters know that a great deal of their time and energy is spent on the subject of boys. Girls are concerned about boys, and at an early age. They have a desire to connect and a willingness to adapt in order to do so. In years past, this adaptability was considered a weakness. This ability to bend, however, is not weakness but resiliency. It comes from valuing relationship over independence. It comes from valuing community over aloneness.

Girls desire to be in relationship with boys. Because of the strength of this desire, one of the first things your daughter may be called upon by God to champion is her own virginity. One of the first arenas your daughter may enter is that of sexual temptation, not necessarily because she wants sex but because she wants intimacy, she wants connection. God, however, wants her to champion His cause of modesty, of abstinence, of marriage. In our society today, this is a huge, encompassing arena and the forces arrayed against your daughter are formidable.

In order to support your daughter, God's champion, to be strong in this area, you need to start early. The first thing you need to do is teach your daughter to value who she is. This is her essence, her core, not the externals. Society wants to focus on the externals, especially for girls. It wants to tell her that her value is found in what she wears, what she weighs, her popularity. In order to drown out this siren's song of appearance, as a parent you must constantly reinforce her inherent value and worth as a person, as a female. This does not mean buying into the lie that in order for a female to have worth she must perform like a male or in the same areas as a male. Help your daughter to be strong by helping her find who she is. Before she can truly cleave to another person, your daughter must first cleave to herself. Help your daughter to love and respect herself. With this kind of inner strength, she'll be able to withstand the pressure to adapt herself sexually in exchange for intimacy.

Parental Preparation

I have worked with so many young girls whose fragile bodies mirrored their fragile souls. For them, their eating disorder was a manifestation of their deep unhappiness and sense of worthlessness. Often, a source of this unhappiness and worthlessness derives from a lack of relationship with their own mothers. It is not a lack of connection they feel to their mothers; on the contrary, it is a lack of relationship. Often, these girls and their mothers are so tightly interconnected, it's difficult to find where one stops and the other starts. The young girl is being suffocated by the control of her mother and uses the eating disorder as an attempt to breathe. She feels she must be perfect in order to be loved, in order to be valued, and will attempt to use the eating disorder to either achieve her distorted view of perfection or numb the pain of never being able to achieve it.

Mothers, you must love and accept your daughters. She was not given to you in order for you to relive your own mistakes. She is not an extension of your personality; she is her own person, sometimes the same and many times different from you. She doesn't need a girlfriend; she needs a mother. She doesn't need a rival; she needs a mother. She doesn't need a saint; she needs a mother.

As her mother, you can help give her the support she needs to explore who she is for herself. She doesn't need to be told who she is; she needs to discover it for herself. If she does not, she will be as susceptible to the thoughts, desires, opinions, and pressures of others as she is to yours. She needs to see you as a guide to her sense of self, not as a danger to it. Otherwise, she'll find ways to distance herself from you, out of sheer self-preservation. In adolescence, you need to be close enough for her to find you without being so close she can't find herself.

Fathers, your job is to love your daughter and value her for being female. She is fascinated by the fact you are male and will judge other males by the relationship she has with you. So make it a good one. If your daughter does not feel a connection to you, she may well seek connection with other males to compensate. This puts her at a severe disadvantage in the sexual arenas of today's culture.

This love and value is tested during your daughter's adolescence. During puberty, as she is physically and emotionally transforming into a woman, these changes can create distance, if you allow it. Puberty is not the time to turn her over to her mother and wait it out until she graduates from high school. Your distance will seem to her like abandonment, like a rejection of her emerging sexuality. Remember, she has a keen desire to exist in relationship, especially as she matures in relationship with the opposite sex. If she does not have a satisfying relationship with you, she may seek it elsewhere.

It is a paradox that teen girls profess the highest degree of independence at one of the most critical times during their lives when they need both mother and father to be actively involved in their lives. She needs you there, not fighting the battles for her but within reach, available for advice, example, and simply to be loved. Adolescence is a time of vast change and she will need the constant of your love as an anchor, as she ventures out further and further into who she is meant to become.

Champions of Family

Women are the heart of the home, of community. Women are meant to be mothers, whether mothering their own children, the children of others, or those who — like children — need defending. One of the main arenas your daughter may be called upon to champion is the arena of family. You must realize that her definition of family may be different from yours. Before she has a family of her own, she may self-define her family. This could be the friends she has chosen to align herself with or a cause she believes in. She has a distinct sense of justice and what's right and will often vocally defend it, even against you. This ability to adopt others into her idea of family is a God-given trait. She, like Him, gathers people to her in order to protect them, looking beyond their shortcomings in the process.

One of my favorite sayings of Jesus has to do with His comparing himself to a rather odd thing. Here He is, the mighty champion of God, creation's agent, yet He compares himself to a common garden fowl, and a hen at that. Luke 13:34 says, "O Jerusalem, Jerusalem, you who kill the prophets and stone those sent to you, how often I have longed to gather your children together, as a hen gathers her chicks under her wings, but you were not willing!" Our daughters will often gather those, even those who have hurt her, under her wings of family. This devotion and selfless love is a mark of Jesus; it is the mark of God's champion. Don't be surprised, therefore, when you see it in your daughter.

Daughters of the King

Remember that it is God who calls His champions into the arenas He has chosen, but He does so without asking them to sacrifice who they are. Let's take a few moments here to look at some of the women highlighted as champions for God in Scripture. Their circumstances and situations can be instructive for us as we seek to support our own daughters.

Deborah

In the Book of Judges, there's an interesting inclusion in the list of judges over the land of Israel, who almost universally are men. However, there is a notable exception. Judges 4:4–5 says, "Now Deborah, a prophetess, the wife of Lappidoth, was judging Israel at that time. And she used to sit under the palm tree of Deborah between Ramah and Bethel in the hill country of Ephraim; and the sons of Israel came up to her for judgment" (NASB). Deborah was empowered by God to enter the arena of judgment, having already proven herself to be His champion in the arena of prophecy.

Judges 4 goes on to say that Deborah also entered the arena of battle, going with Barak into armed conflict with Sisera, the commander of Jabin's army. This was not her idea but Barak's, who refused to enter into battle unless Deborah went with him.

What I want you to recognize from this passage is that God did not call her out of her relationships in order to operate in these arenas. Was she a prophet? Yes! Was she a judge of the nation of Israel? Yes! Did she go into battle for the people of God? Yes! But she was also the wife of Lappidoth. Her relationship with her husband was not negated by God's chosen arenas. He did not ask her to become other than who she was in order to be His champion.

Esther

In many ways, this book is difficult to read for those who grew up on the tenants of feminism. It seems more like a nightmare than a triumph. Esther was a young woman who lived in the land of Israel during a time of occupation. She and all of her people were ruled by King Xerxes, ruler of Persia and Media, or as Esther 1:1 says, "Xerxes who ruled over 127 provinces stretching from India to Cush," Cush referring to the upper Nile region of Egypt. This was a man who ruled over an area from India to Egypt, a powerful man who could pretty much do whatever he chose.

After King Xerxes becomes disenchanted with his current wife, Queen Vashti, over her insubordination to him, he begins a search for a new wife. He issues a decree for all the beautiful virgins in his provinces to be brought to live in his harem. This is not some ancient version of the Miss America pageant. These young women were forcibly taken from their homes, from their families, and sent to live in a distant city, in a king's harem where the only chance of family would be if the king chose to be with them. Otherwise, they were shuttered off, away from view, away from family.

Esther is chosen and brought to the citadel of Xerxes in the city of Susa. Lest you think this was some mark of distinction, listen to what happened to the young women thus taken, from Esther 2:12–14: "Before a girl's turn came to go in to King Xerxes, she had to complete twelve months of beauty treatments prescribed for the women, six months with oil of myrrh and six with perfumes and cosmetics. And this is how she would go to the king: Anything she wanted was given to her to take with her from the harem to the king's palace. In the evening she would go there and in the morning return to another part of the harem to the care of Shaashgaz, the king's eunuch who was in charge of the concubines. She would not return to the king unless he was pleased with her and summoned her by name." Without the protection of marriage, the girl would be summoned to the king as a virgin and leave in the morning a concubine.

Esther, as the story goes, found favor with the king and was chosen not to be his concubine but his wife, but the wife of a pagan king is not like a wife today. If the queen entered the presence of the king without a summons, she could be summarily put to death. In order to save her people from an evil plot to destroy them, Esther risks death by presenting herself to the king and his mercy. By God's grace, she finds favor again with the king, who takes her advice and averts genocide for the people of Israel.

One of the most famous verses from the Book of Esther is found in 4:14, when Esther is fearful of going forward in front of the king and risking death. Her uncle, Mordecai, utters these timeless words: "For if you remain silent at this time, relief and deliverance for the Jews will arise from another place, but you and your father's family will perish. And who knows but that you have come to royal position for such a time as this?" For such a time as this. Esther was God's champion, chosen and positioned carefully by Him for such a time as this.

Esther's purpose was not revealed until a time of great need. Do not be surprised if it seems like your daughter is flowing along with the tide of life. Unknown to you, God may be positioning her right where He wants her, in order to have His champion in place, "for such a time as this." God's arenas are His to determine and His to time.

Dorcas

The world tends to look way up high for champions. God, whose vision is infinite, often looks much closer to home. In the Book of Acts, there is a wonderful story about a woman named Dorcas, or Tabitha. She is described in Acts 9:36 as always doing good and helping the poor. How did she help the poor? Did she organize city-wide food banks or run large charitable organizations? No, again her work was a little bit closer to home. Verse 39 says she did good by making clothing for the poor, one person at a time.

I love this example of Dorcas because it shows how a champion of God can operate right in your own backyard, simply by doing good, in small and measurable ways. For Dorcas, it meant making a robe for someone who needed one. Your daughter may be called upon to be an Esther, on a national stage, or a Dorcas, a neighborhood champion. Now, with our human tendency to place value based on position, it might seem like Esther was much more important than Dorcas. After all, Esther gets an entire book while Dorcas just has a couple of sentences. Was Esther's book bigger than the passage about Dorcas? Yes, but Dorcas was raised from the dead. Esther was positioned to save her people from death. Dorcas' death was positioned to show the power of salvation.

The battle is not ours; it is the Lord's. He is the general and He alone knows the scope of the battle. What we perceive to be a small, insignificant arena may have vast ramifications in the overall plan of God. Help your daughter to view saying yes to the small things that she knows will "do good and help the poor" as victories. Help her to understand that she is no less a champion for God, for finding her arenas close to home.

Trusting the Plan of God

Again, your daughter — as a female champion of God — will enter arenas meant just for her. She will be called upon to champion her own body. She will naturally champion the cause of connection. She will take up the cause of her "family." Your daughter is a natural warrior for these issues. Make sure she is also a champion for God.

At the root of her motivation and reason for battle must be her faith and belief in God. She must have her own relationship with God in order to have wisdom to know which relationships to fight for. To withstand the societal pressures to conform to distorted ideas of female-ness and femininity, she must have a respect and trust for the One who made her that way.

Help your daughter learn to love the fact that God made her female. Help her to learn to appreciate those aspects of herself that are uniquely female. As she enters puberty, give her the support and strength she needs to learn to control her emotions and her hormonal states. These are the essence of who she is and will become as a woman. They were meant to shape her character and teach her how to ride the wave of emotions while staying spiritually buoyant. They were meant to teach her how to seek for anchors within her inner turmoil so she can help others find them in their outer turmoil, truly becoming the anchor of the family herself.

Training Ground

There's one more woman I'd like you to look at for inspiration before we leave this chapter on girls. She doesn't have a name, really. She is called "a wife of noble character" in Proverbs 31:10. The tribute to her character begins in verse 10 and runs through the rest of the chapter. Here is her story:

Proverbs 31

10 A wife of noble character who can find? She is worth far more than rubies.

11 Her husband has full confidence in her and lacks nothing of value.

12 She brings him good, not harm, all the days of her life.

13 She selects wool and flax and works with eager hands.

14 She is like the merchant ships, bringing her food from afar.

15 She gets up while it is still dark; she provides food for her family and portions for her servant girls.

16 She considers a field and buys it; out of her earnings she plants a vineyard.

17 She sets about her work vigorously; her arms are strong for her tasks.

18 She sees that her trading is profitable, and her lamp does not go out at night.

19 In her hand she holds the distaff and grasps the spindle with her fingers.

20 She opens her arms to the poor and extends her hands to the needy.

21 When it snows, she has no fear for her household; for all of them are clothed in scarlet.

22 She makes coverings for her bed; she is clothed in fine linen and purple.

23 Her husband is respected at the city gate, where he takes his seat among the elders of the land.

24 She makes linen garments and sells them, and supplies the merchants with sashes.

25 She is clothed with strength and dignity; she can laugh at the days to come.

26 She speaks with wisdom, and faithful instruction is on her tongue.

27 She watches over the affairs of her household and does not eat the bread of idleness.

28 Her children arise and call her blessed; her husband also, and he praises her:

29 "Many women do noble things, but you surpass them all."

30 Charm is deceptive, and beauty is fleeting; but a woman who fears the Lord is to be praised.

31 Give her the reward she has earned, and let her works bring her praise at the city gate.

If you have a daughter who is old enough, I urge you to sit down with her and read through this incredible description. Talk about the lessons to be learned about this champion of God. Why is she praiseworthy? What about her life is held up for recognition? In this way, you can help your daughter learn what is valuable in God's eyes.

If you don't have a daughter, read this to your son when he is old enough. This is the quality of character he should seek for in a wife. Talk to him about worldly views of what makes a woman beautiful and what God considers beautiful.

If your daughter and your son are young, read this over to yourself. Commit yourself to supporting your daughter to be this kind of champion for God. Accept that God's arenas for her may look very different from the arenas He has in mind for a son. Resist the temptation to ascribe more or less value based upon the arena. God does not and you must not.

Pray for your daughter. Pray for your son's wife. Pray for yourself, as a woman, or for your wife, if a man. Pray for your mother, your sister. Pray for all the women in your life who have taken up the call to arms for God, no matter the arena. And remember, it often takes more courage to battle in obscurity than it does when all the world is watching. In every battle, great and small, the heavenly realm is watching, and waiting for God's champion to declare victory!

Father, I celebrate the women in my life. I thank You for their steadfast example of fighting for what is right. I thank You that you have made women the keepers of the home, of family, of connections. For our daughters, I ask for wisdom and courage. I ask for strength to live out their purpose within the female body You gave them. I ask that You would thwart the plans of the evil one to degrade and devalue women through this culture we live in. Help me to be your champion in this culture, to reject the call to disrespect women, to view them merely as sexual objects. Instead, help me to see each woman I meet through Your eyes. Give each woman I meet the courage to live out her destiny in You. We need champions in this world, Father. We need daughters of faith.

Chapter 11

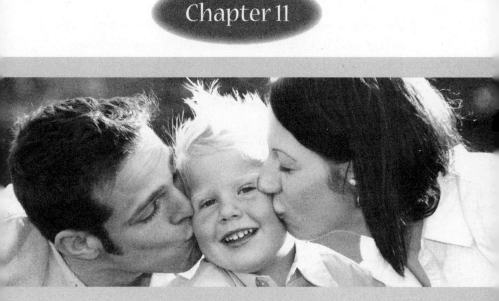

Support for Boys

Listen, my son, to your father's instruction and do not forsake your mother's teaching (Prov. 1:8).

It hasn't been easy being male over the past couple of decades. Say this in a large social gathering and you're likely to be thrown out, unless the social gathering is a group of guys. Our culture today is caught in the midst of a battle between how men used to be perceived, how they are perceived now and how they really should be perceived. Unfortunately, at the same time this battle has been waged, one of the strongest strategies for true understanding — a Judeo-Christian influence — has been vociferously sidelined. In its place, feminism has taken center stage in this cultural clash. Feminism, born of a desire to address basic inequities between men and women, has mutated from "men and women are the same and should be treated the same" to "men should be more like women." Feminism has gone from a philosophy that says in order for women to be considered successful, they must act more like men, to a philosophy that says for men to be considered acceptable, they must act more like women.

This cultural conundrum has serious ramifications for our daughters and our sons. It is damaging to tell girls they need to be like boys in order to be culturally significant. It is also damaging to tell boys that they need to be like girls in order to be socially acceptable. Both assumptions penalize the gender-specific natures given to them by God himself. Again, boys and girls are different. This isn't an egregious social disparity; it is God-designed. As Christians, we must not allow the drumbeat of current cultural thought to drown out the harmony of divine design. Instead, we need to champion God's wisdom ourselves, through the raising of our children. The world may say that there's a battle between the sexes and "a woman needs a man like a fish needs a bicycle," but God says we were made in His image, both male and female, and that "it is not good for the man to be alone" (Gen. 2:18). I choose to go with God on this one.

The Pendulum and the Pit

You might think I'd be jaded, given my line of work, against men. After all, I see the relational damage done by distinct, detached fathers. I see the physical damage done by abusive, violent husbands. I see the emotional damage done by insensitive, selfish fathers and husbands. I see the spiritual damage done by earthly fathers that complicates and clouds an understanding of the heavenly one. I've seen men act like jerks and worse. When I see this type of behavior, I don't ascribe it to masculinity, I ascribe it to sin. When men act in brutish ways, they miss the mark of what God intended for them as men.

Women are not off the hook in the sin department. Please believe me when I tell you I have seen just as much damage done by women as I have by men. Selfishness, manipulation, apathy, and cruelty are not gender-based conditions, they are part of the human condition, which is sinful. We're all in this together. Romans 3:23 clearly states that "all have sinned and fall short of the glory of God." Together we must confront our sin and look to God to transform our thoughts and our lives. It's time to get off the pendulum and stop careening from one cultural misnomer to another. It's time for us to return to a biblical understanding of what it means to be male and female and made in His image.

God made us male and female to help us understand the mystery of intimacy and community. We were made different so we would learn to appreciate how pieces can come together to form a whole. We were designed as two becoming one so we could understand the triune nature of God. Our different genders were meant to draw us closer together. Culture has used those genders to force us apart.

We live in an age where the pendulum of separation is arching over toward a dangerous conclusion. Granted, it's swung wide due to foolishness. This foolishness was the notion that men and women were different and men were superior. This foolishness was based on a male model of the world, which said that men were inherently better than women — stronger physically, more adept intellectually, more solid emotionally. Women's lives and behaviors needed to be monitored and guided. Being a wife was respected, being a mother was respected, but being a woman was not. This was a repugnant, chauvinistic, sexist view of women and it was right for society to reject it.

As often happens, however, in a move to distance itself from this repugnant past, society jumped onto the pendulum of feminism, thinking this would get us to a more equitable place. While the intent was noble, the method was flawed for two reasons: 1) it was based on secular thought not on biblical principles, and 2) feminism didn't know when to stop. We are now at a place in society where men are viewed with suspicion, where male criminal behavior is considered normal and male heroism is noteworthy only for its perceived singularity.

The pendulum didn't stay in the middle for very long. Instead of society getting off at the point where men and women were acknowledged as equal but respected as different, it clung on to the pendulum and just kept right on going. The different and unequal philosophy has been adopted again, but with a pernicious twist: boys and girls are now considered different with boys considered defective. As a culture, we've taken the misdeeds of men and begun to link the violence, insensitivity, and impulsivity that results not with a male nature out of control but with a boy's nature in general.

For a short while, the pendulum slowed and the prevalent cultural paradigm was nature versus nurture. We reached a point of equality, where boys and girls were considered equal, the same. Of course, those observing little boys and little girls couldn't help but point out that, even as small children, they appeared to act quite differently. When put in a room with dolls, little girls picked them up and cuddled them; little boys used them as weapons or projectiles. This is where nature versus nurture came in. We were told that the only reason a little girl cuddled a toy while a little boy threw it was that's what they were taught. Their nature was to act similar; they were taught by society to act differently. Now, however, there is a school of thought that says little girls cuddle toys and little boys throw them because females are inherently loving and gentle, while males are inherently insensitive and violent.

How did full-circle become so warped? In times past, women were considered emotionally unstable because of their feminine nature — their emotional makeup considered volatile and suspect. How did we arrive at a point where men are considered emotionally unstable because of their masculine nature — their physical makeup considered violent and suspect?

There was a time when the differences between little girls and little boys was noted with a smile and a nod, instead of a pointed finger and a shake. If you're old enough, you might remember that nursery rhyme called, "What are little girls made of?" Do you remember how it went? *Sugar and spice and everything nice.* It went on to talk about a male component: What are little boys made of? *Frogs and snails and puppy dog tails.* In our current arch on the pendulum, frogs and snails and puppy dog tails has turned into something much more sinister. Now, boy behavior isn't just different, it's pathological. This thinking is a pit seeking to trap our sons and it must be avoided and argued against.

The Model Student

Nowhere is the pit more evident today than in our educational system. We have traveled from the point where the model student was male and arrived at a point where the model student is now female: compliant, orderly, organized, attentive, verbal. Male students can be somewhat different. Instead of compliant, they can be independent. Instead of orderly, they can demand attention. Instead of organized, they can be forgetful. Instead of attentive, they can be distracted. Instead of verbal, they can be physical. When they are, they aren't defective; it's the nature of their neurology and physiology. Boys, quite frankly, will be boys.

One of the strongest voices for understanding the physical nature of boys, interestingly enough, was mentioned in the last chapter. His name is Michael Gurian and he is the author of *The Wonder of Girls.* He is also the author of several other books, including *The Wonder of Boys, The Good Son, The Minds of Boys,* and *What Stories Does My Son Need?* (More information about these books will appear in the last chapter.) Gurian's contribution to this cultural question has been to explain how the brains and bodies of boys and girls are different. These differences help to explain why girls can be naturally compliant, orderly, organized, attentive, and verbal, while boys can be naturally independent, demanding, forgetful, distracted, and physical.

Simply stated, boys are more physical, more "wiggly," more distracted. They are more kinesthetic, more "hands on." They like to do things instead of being told about things. This isn't insubordinate, it's normal. Too many parents, educators, and health care professionals hanging on to the pendulum say it may be normal, but say it's also pathological and, thus, diagnosable.

The educational system's answer — and that of society at large — to these differences has increasingly been to turn to pharmaceuticals. Look, for example, at the diagnosis of ADD and ADHD in children today. The majority of children diagnosed are boys. It seems that all of a sudden being a boy is considered a state to be medicated. Instead of altering our classrooms and educational delivery models to be more conducive to male learning patterns, we have decided it's just a whole lot easier to medicate our males. This isn't to say that every boy in the classroom is on Ritalin or some other behavior-adjusting drug but the majority of those who take them are male. The majority of those in special education class are male. Males drop out of school more often than girls. College is increasingly becoming the domain of women. Boys grow up to be men who feel marginalized and confused about their place in society. Their growth as males, including spiritual growth, can be tentative and stunted.

This has serious consequences for God's champions, the sons under our roofs. God's plans and societal priorities are already at serious odds, in so many ways. What happens to our boys when they feel called by God not only to be a champion but a male-champion in a world where that model is considered flawed? This constitutes a barrier to our sons achieving their God-designed destiny. We must fortify our sons and help them leap over those barriers — to gain the prize God has in store for them.

Boys to Men

Society does not support a Christian view of manhood, of male championship. It hasn't for over 30 years and, unless something dramatic happens, does not appear destined to change anytime soon. So, prepare yourself to buck the tide. In order for your son to learn what it means to be a man and God's champion, you need to provide a supportive environment, a place for your son to learn what it means to be a man and more — a godly man.

Band of Brothers

In the last chapter, I said I was a male in a sea of females. As a male, at times it can be a little overwhelming. That's why I am so grateful for the men who are a constant part of my life. First and foremost is my dad, Larry. I am so fortunate that he is a constant part of my life and the lives of my sons. I love and respect my dad and know he feels the same way about me. He accepts me as a man, a husband, a father, a business owner, in my own right. In so many ways, over all the years of my life, my father has affirmed me. He also taught me about hard work, integrity, compassion, and loyalty.

After I left home and went to college, I was blessed to find a mentor at my church, University Presbyterian, Dr. Bruce Larson, the pastor. During my clinical internship, I was pleased to be mentored by Dr. Arden Snyder, at Virginia Mason Hospital. Their influence gave me direction to start my first counseling practice over 20 years ago.

Over the years at the Center, I've been around many dedicated, professional male colleagues who have partnered together with me in the cause of whole-person healing and recovery. I consider them my "band of brothers" in the battlefield of mental health counseling and chemical dependency treatment with Christian principles.

I've also been blessed to know and worship with several other area pastors who have shown me the resilience needed to spread the love of Christ in the most unchurched region of the country — the Pacific Northwest.

As you think of your sons, who are their role models? When they look around to see how it works to be a man today, who do they see? Moreover, with whom can they come alongside? Who can they work with, walk with, and talk with, about what it means to be a man? Naturally, I take the role of father seriously, but I also recognize that my sons will need more than just me to show them what it means to be a man. Who will be their "band of brothers" growing up? Who will be their male mentors?

In order to support your son in growing up to be the champion God intends, start now to identify and support male mentors and male associates. These could be fellow dads of your child's classmates in school. They could be coaches and teachers. Within your faith community, these men can act as older brothers, surrogate fathers, uncles, and grandfathers. The wider the age range of these men, the greater the opportunity your son will have to see how men act and interact at various stages in their lives.

First and foremost, fathers need to be accessible to their children. If you are living apart from your son, you must make the commitment to maintain ties. You must spend as much time as possible with your son, even if this means you must make personal and work sacrifices. Your son needs you, your presence in his life, your wisdom in dealing with circumstances, your direction in making decisions, and your example in being a man. There is no substitute for you in his life, but he'll find one if you don't fulfill this sacred responsibility.

Sadly, there are too many circumstances where fathers do not remain connected to their sons. If you are a single mother reading this book, it will be up to you — up to you to help provide your son with male leadership and mentoring, not try to be a father yourself. As his mother, you cannot also be his father. This is also a myth perpetuated by the feminist movement — that children need mothers but fathers are optional. Studies are quite definitive about the deleterious effects of children growing up without a father. They, quite simply, are at higher risk from more difficulties in school to higher commissions of crimes to greater rates of incarceration. All children, not just sons, need the presence of both mothers and fathers in their lives. What was called the nuclear family — a father, a mother, and children — is the best model for raising healthy children. If part of your family is lacking, look around you — to extended family, friends, and faith community — to fill in the gaps.

The Power of Male Bonding

The Bible is full of stories depicting the power of male bonding. While this has been derided in our culture as just an excuse to work on cars or drink beer and watch football, there is power when men come together. As your son matures, he needs time to engage in male bonding and he'll find a way to do this, even without your help. How many times have you seen young boys band together and put out a figurative or literal "no girls allowed" sign? They will withdraw, in order to spend time with other boys. This could be through organized sports teams, clubs at school, even groups of neighborhood kids.

Boys will often organize themselves around an activity or pursuit in order to spend time together. Within the context of the group, they find validity and significance. They're a part of a club, a team, or a group. You want your son to be involved with groups that encourage and support your Christian beliefs and his emerging faith. For this reason, it's important for you to know who your son's friends are. Within the group setting, there is pressure to conform to the will of the group.

Boys will find other boys to bond with. If chosen unwisely, this group may be a gang or one formed around criminal intent, such as obtaining and using drugs. It is within the context of the group that a boy validates his maleness. If the group is centered around violence, his initiation will be violent. If it is centered around drugs, he will begin to use drugs himself. The pull of the pack is powerful in boys and you must be aware of it, as a parent.

It is not realistic for you to pick out your son's friends. However, you can make sure that your son has access to other boys in the neighborhood whose families share your values if not your specific faith. You can commit to taking your son to Bible class and youth group at your church or faith community. Encourage your son to have his friends over to the house. If he doesn't want you to meet them, be concerned and investigate further.

For our boys, LaFon and I make sure they are involved in a musical activity and a sports activity. Music is intellectually and creatively engaging and sports is physically and socially engaging. Given the physicality of boys, it makes perfect sense for your son to get involved in sports. Not only will he be learning about baseball, basketball, soccer, or tennis, for example, he'll be interacting and learning from the other boys on the team, and from the men who act as coaches and helpers.

Again, as your son gets older, he'll begin to self-select his own mentors. Often, these are chosen on the basis of vocation. In my case, Dr. Larson became my mentor because of our joint passion for ministry to the hurting. He has remained influential in my life, even though we no longer are in close contact.

This example of male bonding and mentoring is certainly echoed in Scripture. Moses mentored Joshua. David bonded to Jonathan. Paul mentored Timothy. John bonded to Jesus. There is a wonderful proverb about this process that says, "As iron sharpens iron, so one man sharpens another" (Prov. 27:17). The connection and love that grows between men is a powerful force. At its best, it encourages openness, honesty, accountability, and perseverance.

When thinking about the power of male friendship and companionship, of course, Jonathan and David come to mind. First Samuel 18:3 says, "And Jonathan made a covenant with David because he loved him as himself." This friendship was made all the more difficult as David was destined to replace Jonathan's father, Saul, as leader over Israel. The devotion of Jonathan to David and vice versa is a powerful testimony to male bonding and love, even in difficult circumstances. I think of the type of connection forged among soldiers, police, and firefighters, who will sacrifice their own lives to save their friends.

Elijah and Elisha

To find an example of the power of male mentoring, I have always liked the story of Elijah and Elisha. Their story begins in 1 Kings 19, in verse 16, when God commands Elijah to anoint Elisha, son of Shaphat, to succeed him as God's prophet. In essence, God chose who was going to take over Elijah's "family business." What is impressive to me is the mutual respect and love that grows between these two men. We don't know how old Elisha was when Elijah called him, but he was old enough to be plowing with oxen and young enough to want to kiss his father and mother goodbye (1 Kings 19:19–20). He leaves his parents and follows Elijah, to become "his attendant." While the rest of 1 Kings is full of the mighty deeds of Elijah, you don't hear about Elisha again until the second chapter of 2 Kings, just prior to Elijah being taken up by the Lord. Knowing that his time to leave this earth was near, Elijah kept instructing Elisha to separate from him. Three times Elisha said no, understanding that he would not see Elijah again. When Elijah was finally taken up in a chariot of fire and a whirlwind, Elisha's words were not of awe at this unprecedented event, but of personal anguish, "My father! My father!" he cries and tears his clothing in sorrow.

Elijah's relationship was now like a father to a son, with all the resulting emotional connection. Did this mean that Elisha no longer loved his own father? I don't believe so! Elisha didn't reject his own father in order to love Elijah; he had the great fortune to love and be loved by two important men in his life. The mentors of our sons add to their relationships, not take away from ours.

Elijah had been taken away from Elisha but his influence over Elisha remained. God granted Elisha's wish to receive a double portion of Elijah's spirit. Elisha went on to accomplish great deeds and miracles, as had Elijah, throughout his life. These deeds are recorded throughout the book of 2 Kings, until the passage that tells of his death in 2 Kings 13:20. Elisha dedicates his life to acting out his ministry, his purpose, as Elijah did.

Mentoring is an age-old tradition. In the New Testament, Jesus mentors the 12 disciples and they leave family and jobs and follow Him, making His cause their cause, His life their life. As you mold God's champion, your son, you must be prepared for the possibility that God will call your son to leave you and enter into deep relationship with another man or group of men. I think of the sons of Zebedee, James and John. Once called by Jesus, they leave their father's business, his life, and go off to follow Jesus.

In the same way, the course of obedience for your son to God may require him to leave you. It may require him to leave the family business, even if you've always envisioned him taking your place some day. Again, your son is not your own; he belongs to God and God may have a completely different business or arena for your son to operate in. You prepare your son by helping him mature and grow, and then you let him go. This separation is vital to his becoming a man in his own right.

Male Milestones

All of us need traditions and markers in life, times when we stop long enough to take note and celebrate a significant event. These can be spontaneous celebrations or planned events. The one that comes to mind easiest is the Jewish tradition of a bar mitzvah, when a male child turns 13. This is the age at which a male child is considered old enough to be accountable to the commandments. "Bar" means "son" and "mitzvah" means "commandment." At this age, he becomes "a son of the commandment" and has the right to take part in leading a religious ceremony, to be counted as an adult male Jew. This was needed for the purpose of obtaining a quorum of ten in order to be allowed to recite certain prayers. As an adult Jewish male, he was able to enter into contracts, give testimony in a religious court, and to marry. This happens at age 13, whether there is a ceremony or not, but every Jewish family I know makes both a bar mitzvah and a bat mitzvah (for girls at age 12) a family event.

As Christians, we don't have a similar time-line. Our children come to faith at different ages, depending upon their maturity and spiritual growth. I hope all of us, as Christians, however, make sure to mark our child's moment of decision, when he or she makes a decision to follow Christ.

I like the idea of tradition and initiation. I do not like, however, the practice of hazing. When milestones are celebrated, they should be done with integrity and dignity in mind, supporting a difficult decision or feat with respect and affirmation. Every family must find ways to affirm their sons through tradition and initiation. Maybe it's a yearly father-son camp-out, or running in a racing event to-gether, or climbing a mountain. It is not by accident that many of these events include physical acts of perseverance and stamina. Boys — and men, for that matter — need to be challenged. They need to be challenged physically, emotionally, and spiritually. In this way, they learn to jettison their old fears of who they are and what they can accomplish, and replace them with a new understanding of just how far they can reach. These initiations are meaningful when done with other males, who can encourage them to continue on, to trust in themselves, to persevere, when things get tough.

The Ministry of Men

Another thing these times of male bonding do is celebrate not only an event but just the fact of being male. Especially in our culture today, it's great to have time together when you don't have to apologize for doing something typically male. It's relaxing to get together with a group of men and enjoy a shared activity. At our church, we have a wonderful men's ministry. This is so vital for young Christian men, who may not have had the benefit of a father growing up. This ministry allows men to bond together and form spiritual mentoring relationships. Older men in the church can help younger men learn not only what it means to be a man, a husband, and a father, but how to be a Christian man, a Christian husband, a Christian father. This is a challenge of a different sort.

If your faith community does not have a men's ministry — and you're a man — why not start one? Talk to other men in your congregation and decide to meet together, even if it doesn't start out as anything as formal as a "ministry." If you're a man without children, look around your congregation. Surely you'll be able to find a fatherless boy who would benefit from your involvement in his life, through the structure of a men's ministry. In the secular world, this is called "Big Brothers." In the church, it's called fellow-ship. Be prepared, however, to undergo a certain level of suspicion if you express interest in being involved in the life of a young boy, even in the church. There is a fear of predators and your life must demonstrate your commitment to living a godly life. Be wise about the types of activities you choose. Be open, transparent, and engage in group events or activities. Prove yourself worthy and trustworthy to mentor another male.

If you are a mother of a fatherless son who is young, look around your circle of male friends, acquaintances, and Christian brothers. If your son is older, help him become involved in the men's ministry at your church or encourage him to form a mentoring relationship with an older Christian brother. We need to be available to each other. The church is the family of God and a place of support and strength to His emerging champions.

Gaining Control of Self

So, whether you're a father, an uncle, a friend, or a mentor, what do you teach this young male about what it is to be a man? You will most certainly teach by your example, which is a daunting prospect in itself! Your job is not to be perfect, because you can't be, but rather to model how to be a man and a believer in this world. You would not be doing your job well if you did not take the stumbles you have in life to model the importance of repentance and forgiveness. After all, this was Christ's overriding message, and it is completely appropriate for you to pass on to the boys and young men in your own life.

Your life is an open book your son will read, and learn about himself and about God. Because of this, what you do and how you live are important. You want to do the right thing as often as you're able. You want to use the opportunities that arise to instill God's Word deep into the heart of your son. These are words for a champion to live by, to conquer the world for Christ.

The world is fully prepared to teach your son what it means to be a secular man — how to take foolish risks, treat other people with contempt, compete in order to dominate, view women from a sexual lens, live for today and ignore the consequences. Just look at the television ads on stations that cater predominantly to men. These messages are out there and pervasive. As God's champion, your son needs a different curriculum.

Fortunately, knowing this, God prepared another champion long ago to chronicle important words of wisdom you can pass down to your son. (An important side benefit is as you are teaching your son, you are relearning yourself!) The Bible says that "All scripture is God-breathed and is useful for teaching, rebuking, correcting and training in righteousness" (2 Tim. 3:16). It's appropriate to use the entire Bible to teach your child about how to be a champion. The people of Scripture provide powerful examples of how to live and how not to live.

There is a book, however, I've found very important, especially as I think about teaching my sons. It's the Book of Proverbs. I guess I like it because it's written from a father to his son. I feel a connection there, and it's full of immensely practical truths about life. They're the kind of things found in every day life that I can use as examples, understandable even to children. Now, granted, I'm not going to start out my six-year-old with admonitions about adultery, but I plan to make sure he understands sexual purity at the appropriate age!

Proverbs is basically a compilation of wise sayings but, at its heart, it's wisdom mostly from one man, Solomon, to his son — and to our sons, by extension. It begins with an explanation of its purpose: "The proverbs of Solomon son of David, king of Israel: for attaining wisdom and discipline; for understanding words of insight; for acquiring a disciplined and prudent life, doing what is right and just and fair; for giving prudence to the simple, knowledge and discretion to the young — let the wise listen and add to their learning, and let the discerning get guidance — for understanding proverbs and parables, the sayings and riddles of the wise." I cannot think of a better goal as a father for my sons — I want Gregg and Benjamin to attain wisdom and discipline; to have understanding and insight of themselves, of God and the world; to live a disciplined and prudent life; to do what is right and just and fair; to learn to be prudent when they don't know something and to accept guidance and knowledge even though young and even when old; to understand what the Scriptures say and mean. I cannot think of a better definition of a champion of God.

Champions are meant to conquer, to enter a field of battle, to be courageous and unafraid. This is the dream of most boys and most men, if they are honest. This kind of bravado is necessary to overcome doubt and obstacles. This kind of bravado can also lead to boasting and self-reliance. That's why I love the sentiment of the very next verse in Proverbs 1:7: "The fear of the LORD is the beginning of knowledge, but fools despise wisdom and discipline." This verse tells me something important about God's champions: they are to fear God and seek after wisdom and discipline.

Wisdom and discipline are not gained overnight. They are not handed to us in a beautifully wrapped box. They are not like a gift or a talent, for which we have a natural tendency. They are gained through practice and diligence. This is the sort of spiritual challenge your son can embrace, and will embrace if you communicate its value and your commitment to its teaching.

These are lessons well spent. Here are just a few for you to teach your son:

- Self-reliance is a male trait. Independence and risk-taking are part of the male make-up. Therefore it's important to teach your son that he is not the sole decider of what's best in his life. Proverbs 3:5 will remind him to: "Trust in the LORD with all your heart and lean not on your own understanding." Proverbs 28:26 puts it this way: "He who trusts in himself is a fool, but he who walks in wisdom is kept safe." It is important to recognize your own shortcomings and take steps to minimize them.

- The physical nature of boys can lead to a temptation to use that physicality to harm others for selfish gain. This temptation is seen in full flower in today's prison population, which is overwhelmingly male. Proverbs 1:11–18 makes a persuasive argument that such deeds lead only to self-destruction, not self-fulfillment.

- Males are created with strong hormonal imperatives and sexual desires. If indulged in, they can lead to sexual immorality, which is condemned in no uncertain terms in Scripture. With our over-sexualized culture, there are few voices teaching abstinence and sexual purity. (Please see the last chapter for a description of my book, *Too Close to the Flame: Recognizing and Avoiding Sexualized Relationships.*) Proverbs 2:16–18, as well as many other passages in Proverbs, uncovers the truth of sexual immorality and its eternal consequence — spiritual death. Our boys need to be taught the value of sexual purity and respect for their virginity — sadly a term more often associated with our daughters than our sons.

- Male impulsivity can lead to problems other than sexual promiscuity. It can cause boys to say things they later wish they shouldn't. James will later go on to talk about the need to tame the tongue, but there are valuable lessons on this in Proverbs 10:19 and 17:27. When tempers flare, it's easy for words to incite escalation. Our sons need to learn how to control their tempers and their tongues.

- Even with more and more women entering the work force, men need to be prepared to be income providers, for themselves, certainly, as well as for their families. Because of this, our sons need to learn the value of diligence and hard work. These attributes are heralded in Proverbs 6:6; 10:4–5; and 20:13, to name a few.

- Males in our culture still hold positions of power, even with the influence of feminism. There is a temptation to use that position for selfish gain, instead of to protect others. As we've seen in the terrible financial scandals of the past few years, there are some men in power who use that power to enrich themselves at the expense of others. Champions of God may very well be placed by God into positions of power. For this reason, Proverbs 31:4–5 is an important lesson for our sons: "It is not for Kings, O Lemuel — not for kings to drink wine, not for rulers to crave beer, lest they drink and forget what the law decrees, and deprive all the oppressed of their rights." Leaders are to protect those under their care, not exploit them.

- It used to be that men in power were frowned upon if they acted arrogantly. Now, with the advent of million-dollar sports stars, humility has taken a bit of a beating. (That's why I'm so proud of my brother, Shaun Alexander, and the way he conducts himself in public and in private.) Proverbs teaches a valuable lesson about the value of humility and the outcome of being too proud in 11:2, 16:18, and 21:24.

- While both genders abuse alcohol, males constitute a higher percentage of those convicted of drunk driving. In crimes of domestic violence, often alcohol is involved, as it is in acts of violence in general. Proverbs is quite specific on the outcome of becoming addicted to alcohol. Proverbs 20:1 puts it pretty succinctly: "Wine is a mocker and beer a brawler; whoever is led astray by them is not wise." Even though Proverbs 23:29–35 was written long, long ago, it's depiction of the life of an alcoholic is no less true today. For over 20 years, the Center has provided treatment for those addicted to alcohol and other drugs. I've seen the devastation it produces in individuals and families. You can be sure my sons will hear these wise words from Proverbs!

- As a husband, a father, and a business owner, it can often seem as if I'm in charge of my own destiny, and in many things, that's true. But, it's important for me, who has such influence over those around me, to remember that I may have a position of power in this life but I am ultimately accountable to God. Men are often in control and enjoy control. Again, the temptation exists to misuse that control. As we train up our young champions for God, we must teach them to handle control and power well, and to realize that God is in control of their lives and actions. This important lesson is brought home in Proverbs 5:21, 15:3, 16:9, and 20:4.

Training Ground

Your son is a precious gift from God. His masculinity is intentional and created by God for His plans and purposes. Do not allow the world to emasculate your son, through its suspicion and disrespect for men. This is a current societal phenomenon and one that must be resisted. To be healthy and whole, our sons need to embrace their masculinity. As a parent, you must be aware of any influences that seek to demean your son's gender. Teach your son about what it means to be male, the special plans God intends for him — as man, as husband, as father, as protector and defender of the weak and powerless. Teach your son it is perfectly appropriate for him to see himself as a hero, as a warrior, as a champion. Help him to expand his vision to whatever form God intends for his life.

For fathers, I'd like you to take some time and honestly evaluate the amount of time you're spending with your son, and the quality of that time. Do you make time in your week to stop and talk to your son? Do you play together? Do you engage in a hobby together? As you look at your life, what lessons are you teaching your son? How often do you engage him in spiritual discussions? Are you teaching him to be a man — or a man of God?

It's time for you to do some soul searching. Have you been ashamed about your gender, yourself? How has the past 30 years or so of feminism's influence on our culture influenced you? What changes do you need to make in order to emulate a more mature man of God to your son?

For mothers, what attitudes about males are you communicating to your son? Do you show a preference for female solutions and attitudes over male ones? Have you bought into the myth that boys should be more like girls? How has the past 30-plus years affected you? How do you feel about men? How do you feel about your own father? Your own husband? Your own son? Whether you intend to, or not, you are teaching your son about men by your attitudes toward them.

I encourage you — male or female — to read two important books about boys, after you finish this one, of course! One I've already mentioned, *The Wonder of Boys* by Michael Gurian. The other is by the noted Christian author and teacher Dr. James Dobson, and is called *Bringing Up Boys* (information on these books will appear in the last chapter). Both of these books are written with a clear understanding of the differences in boys and girls and a celebration of the differences. Get to know how the mind and body of your son works.

Father, thank You for my son. Help me to know how to raise him as a man of God. Protect him from the influences of this world that seek to emasculate the nature You designed in him. Allow his strength of character and purpose to expose the lies told about males. Help him to be a champion for Your design and creation of gender. Where I fail to understand him, give me knowledge. Where I fail to teach him, give me wisdom. Where I fail to love him, grant me forgiveness. When I need to release him, help me let him go to become the man You intend.

Chapter 12

Support
Across the Ages

Like a warrior's fistful of arrows are the children of a vigorous youth. Oh, how blessed are you parents, with your quivers full of children! Your enemies don't stand a chance against you; you'll sweep them right off your doorstep (Ps. 127:4–6; TM).

My children are small and, when I am out with them in public, it can sometimes seem like a battle. As I've said, we often go to Mariners and Seahawks games in Seattle — and we're not alone. Usually, I'm navigating two small heads through a sea of literally thousands of people, most of whom are bigger and taller. Gregg, at six, is too old to hold Dad's hand.

Benjamin, at three, is too independent to hold Dad's hand. So, I do my best to herd them through the crowds, watching for openings, alert to potential dangers. I never forget when I'm at a game that I'm a spectator but I'm also a parent, which according to the Scripture above means a warrior for my children. I'm watching the game but I'm also watching out for my kids.

This book is about watching out for your kids. It's about doing everything you can to mold God's champion in your child. I hope you've also realized it's about molding another of God's champions — you. That theme — of parent as warrior for their children — is why I love Psalm 127:4–6 in The Message by Eugene Peterson quoted at the beginning of this chapter. The word picture it portrays from Scripture is so true: a parent is a warrior in his or her own right. The parent, a warrior, raises up children as warriors, and with the strength of the family together, enemies are swept "right off your doorstep." We raise our children to be champions to strengthen our physical family now and to strengthen our spiritual family for eternity. It's important to recognize that our children, when fully formed as God champions, may be the very ones God sends to defend us when we're in danger.

I guess it makes me go back to Mary, the mother of Jesus. Parents, mothers especially, are recognized as fearless defenders of their children. I can't imagine Mary and Joseph were any different, as Jesus was growing up. While we don't have many accounts of Jesus as a boy, there is one recounted in Luke 2:41–52. This is where Jesus, at 12, accompanies His parents, friends, and extended family to Jerusalem for Passover. At the end of the Feast, the group heads off home but after a day of walking, Mary and Joseph realize Jesus is missing. After frantically searching, they head back to Jerusalem to search. Of course, they find Jesus, but only after three days of searching. I cannot imagine the anxiety of missing a child. It's one reason I keep a sharp eye on my kids every time we're out in public.

Upon finding Jesus in the temple courts, Mary asks the timeless parent question — "Son, why have you treated us like this? Your father and I have been anxiously searching for you" (Luke 2:48). The

Scriptures don't record an exclamation point, but every time I read it, I sure imagine one there. It's a question borne of fear and frustration.

Jesus, at 12, was busy being molded into God's champion. This champion would go on to conquer death and sin. In raising Jesus as God's champion, Mary and Joseph were raising up their own redeemer. I cannot tell you the number of times I've worked with families in trouble, where it is the daughter or son of that family who hoists the red flag — often by their own challenging behavior — that sounds an alert to the dangers the family faces. These sons and daughters, by screaming out for help, bring amazing healing, reconciliation, and grace to the entire family. By demanding that someone stop and take notice of the problems in the family, they break down the walls of silence and allow healing into the family. Now, I'm not saying that is the case in every family, but I do know that children in the family can be used by God to strengthen and defend that family. This is why it's so important for us as parents to take our job of supporting these champions very seriously, for we never know but what one of the first arena's God calls them to may be no farther than the family doorstep.

Support Across the Ages

It's easy to see ourselves as warriors, as guardians over our children when they are young. They are so vulnerable and innocent. At night, when I look in on my sleeping boys, I'm struck by the intensity of emotions I feel for them. I don't ever want anything to harm my children. When I look at them, I do feel like a warrior.

Our children, though, need us to be warriors for them throughout their entire childhood and adolescence. They need us to support them, as champions for God, not only when they're young and vulnerable but also when they're older and vulnerable. Granted, as they age, they're gaining the skills and insights they need to transition into their championship role, but we must not pull our support too soon.

I'd like us to look at the support we can give our children in four different ages — birth to 5, 5 to 12, 12 to 16, and 16 to 21. Each stage has its own advantages and challenges for supporting God's growing champion. Especially in the latter two stages, it can be helpful to remember Psalm 127:4–6 and say over and over to yourself, "Yes, my child is a blessing; yes, my child is a blessing; yes, my child is a blessing."

Ages Birth to 5

This is a foundational stage for the molding of God's champion in your home, for how you view your child will become his or her dominant view of self. At this age, your child uses your world view as a filter for everything he or she sees. This may be difficult to imagine when your three year old is loudly rejecting your world view in the grocery store but it's true, nonetheless. What you think matters to young children, so you need to be careful how you're communicating. Ask yourself the following questions, as you deal with your young child:

What do my words convey? Your words must set your child's self-identity.

- *You are a blessing.* Your child must know through your words that you consider him or her to be a gift from God, a blessing from the Lord. Remember, your infant may not understand all of the words you use but they rapidly understand, much more and much faster than we sometimes give them credit for. Choose your words well. Is your child a gift and a blessing — or a problem and a bother? How do you speak to your child? How do you speak about your child to others? I can assure you that most children early on in this stage know their name and are sensitive to it.

- *You are special.* Children need to understand they are special, set apart, with a unique destiny pre-ordained by God. The theme verse for this is 1 Peter 2:9: "But you are a chosen people, a royal priesthood, a holy nation, a people belonging to God, that you may declare the praises of him who called you out of darkness into his wonderful light." Your child is special and needs to understand this amazing fact. To hide this from your son or daughter is like hoarding a priceless gift, meant for them.

- *You are different.* You must tell your child that he or she is different from the rest of the world. This is not a negative thing to convey to children. During this stage of life they are already learning about many differences — who is and who is not family, gender differences, differences in moods, desires, and wants. You are teaching this young champion the concept of *allegiance*. When aligned with God, your child will be different from the world.

- *You belong to God.* As parents, you can convey this amazing revelation through an emphasis on how much God loves your child. You can speak about the family of God and how your child is a part and you are a part. Children understand first the immediate family—mommy, daddy, siblings. Then, they realize there are more family — grandparents, aunts, uncles, cousins. Your words can help them understand God has a family, a special family chosen just by Him and your child is a part of it.

What do my actions convey? It does no good to say a thing if you don't live it, if your actions don't back up your words. Children at this age are very literal. They, after all, go through that hysterical phase where they think if they don't see you, you don't see them. From this logical sequencing comes that wonderful game of peek-a-boo. Children are logical — at least in their realm of experience. Their brains are connecting simple and complex truths about themselves and about the world. Make sure your words and your actions don't produce a dichotomy and appear illogical. In cases such as these, actions really do speak louder than words. You can undo a positive thing you've said by a negative thing you've done. As a sinful man, I wish this wasn't so, but it is and I must accept it and factor this into my actions. In the privacy of my home, the world may not be watching, but my children are. My private actions must be in alignment with my private and public words.

What does my life convey? Children this age need time. I've spoken about this in depth earlier in the book, but I want to reiterate it here. Your child is going to look at the content of your life and come up with conclusions about what you consider important, what you consider unimportant, and how he or she fits into all of that. If you say your child is a blessing and valuable but always seem to have excuses for not being together, what does that convey? If you say your child is special but consistently overlook the things your child needs or values, what does that convey? If you say your life should be different from the world but he or she can see no outward signs of that, you call yourself a liar. If you say your child belongs to God but do not engage your child in spiritual activities such as church attendance, Bible reading, and prayer, your child won't understand what belonging to God really means. All of these things take time to convey. They take your decision and your consistency. Your life is your child's litmus test. This is so important. Do everything you can to make sure it turns out positive for the Lord.

What does my heart convey? Children long to know the heart of their parents, just as David longed to know God's heart. We must, therefore, be willing to open up our hearts to our children. At this tender age, children are drawn to the love, care, and compassion of their parents. If we are distant and distracted emotionally and physically from our children at this age, we damage their ability to understand the true loving nature of their Heavenly Father. Why should they align themselves as a champion to someone who doesn't seem to care about them? The world will lure them away, to champion its causes and concerns, if they are not firmly attached to God. It's not just what you say about your children or what you do for your children that matters; it's also about what you *feel* for your children. Words can be chosen, actions can be planned, but feelings are revealed. Make sure what your heart reveals to your child is your belief in his or her being and becoming a champion for God.

Ages 5 to 12

These years used to be thought of as the elementary school years. When I was growing up, five was the age you started school. Now, even Benjamin, at three, is in preschool. But I still think there's something special about the beginning of kindergarten. This is the stage where the influences of others begin to have a significant pull on the hearts and minds of children. This is the age where they begin to have opportunity to demonstrate some of the skills they've been learning. They're carefully beginning to flap their wings a bit; they're not nearly ready to leave the nest but they're starting to test out how it feels to use those wings within the safety of the family.

This is also a very important time spiritually for children. They are gaining the intellectual understanding and emotional maturity to grasp spiritual concepts. This is the age where children come to grips with the shattering truth that people, even good people, sin. They learn about the sacrifice of Christ on the Cross and why this was necessary. While up to this age children are generally taught how much Jesus loves them, during this stage they begin to learn at what cost. Some children will make lifelong spiritual commitments at this age. As parents, we can sometimes doubt their level of commitment or their ability to understand what this means. We think to ourselves, this child hasn't even mastered quadratic equations, how can he or she possibly respond to the most fundamental mystery of the universe? The answer, of course, has nothing to do with mathematics and everything to do with faith. A child at this age is capable of immense faith and commitment to God.

Let's go back to our story about Jesus. It was at age 12 that He was compelled to remain in Jerusalem, while the rest of the entourage left. His desire was to listen to what the Scriptures had to say and to ask questions of the teachers there. In our culture, if a 12 year old stayed at church for three days, we would call the authorities. In Jesus' day, even though the temple leaders in many ways were the authority of the day, I imagine it was still unusual. There was something about His demeanor and eagerness to learn that was communicated to the teachers. The Scriptures say, "Everyone who heard him was amazed at his understanding and his answers" (Luke 2:47). He was young but he was also spiritual at age 12.

We talked earlier about Moses' sister Miriam. We know that she was older than Moses when he was put by his mother in the reed basket and sent down the river to save his life from the Egyptians. Miriam was older, but she was still a child and probably within this age range. Miriam was a Hebrew, a slave; she had to be careful in a society where she had no standing whatsoever. Her brother Moses, by decree, was supposed to be killed. Even though it meant a degree of danger on her part, she just couldn't let her little brother float off down the river without watching to see what happened. This pint-sized child grew up to be a mighty witness and champion for God in later life, but no more so than when she was young.

What about Isaac? We herald the faith of Abraham, and rightly so, in obeying God's command to sacrifice his son, born to him when he was 100 years old. Hebrews 11:17–19 says, "By faith Abraham, when God tested him, offered Isaac as a sacrifice. He who had received the promises was about to sacrifice his one and only son, even though God had said to him, 'It is through Isaac that your offspring will be reckoned.' Abraham reasoned that God could raise the dead, and figuratively speaking, he did receive Isaac back from death." Abraham had the faith to sacrifice his son; Isaac had the faith to be sacrificed. Earlier in the story, Isaac, questioning this trip he's on with his dad, asks where they will find the lamb for the sacrifice. After all, he sees the wood, he sees the fire — he knows the drill — where's the lamb? Abraham answers that God will provide. Knowing this, Isaac, when the time comes, is bound by his father and placed on the altar. He's a child, but he's not an ignorant one. Certainly, when he sees the knife raised above him, he knows he is the one to be killed. Yet Isaac does not try to get away (which probably wouldn't be that hard for a child dealing with a 100-plus-year-old man — sometimes I can barely keep up with my three year old!). Abraham had faith, but so did Isaac, in a most profound way in the midst of a traumatic event.

Can I tell you that I've seen this kind of faith and courage demonstrated in my own life? I've seen it in my own kids and in your kids, too. Children often are able to understand and express basic spiritual truths, even in the midst of traumatic circumstances. Their faith, sadly and brilliantly, is often the only thing that carries them through, when dealing with the monumental failure of the adults in their lives to care for and protect them.

As parents, we tend to discount spiritual insight because it comes in a smaller package. But, as parents, don't you really know otherwise?

I am quite certain that each one of you has heard and observed your child understanding or espousing a deep spiritual truth. One night recently, while preparing to say his prayer before going to bed, Gregg looked at me and said, "When I go to heaven, I'm going to ask God if I can live again since it's so much fun." It struck me, as an adult, how many times I'd really thought that myself. Gregg understands some foundational spiritual truths — at six — that he is going to heaven, that God will be available in heaven to speak to, that God will be approachable in heaven and interested in what he has to say and ask, and that God is in charge of both this life and the next. As a kid, he realizes it's pretty fun down here.

For ages 5 through 12, you continue to teach your child that he or she is a blessing, is special, is different, and belongs to God, but you add the opportunities for your child to demonstrate that understanding. You acknowledge the ways your child is growing in wisdom in God, just like Jesus and Miriam and Isaac. You accept that God is working mightily in your child, in ways you have no control over, and you accept the arenas God calls your children to.

One more thing — you add your perspective on these situations for your child. Even when Mary and Joseph became angry at Jesus for staying behind in Jerusalem, this was a perspective He needed to hear. It allowed Him to demonstrate His spiritual maturity by reminding His parents they should have looked for Him in the temple in the first place! When Moses' mother placed her son in a basket and sent him floating off down a river, she surely must have explained her reasoning to his older sister Miriam. You can bet that Abraham and Isaac had a long discussion after the miracle at the altar and the angel of the Lord staying Abraham's hand.

When your child undergoes a significant event or reveals a spiritual insight, accept it for the miracle of faith it is but don't treat it with "kid gloves." Talk about it with your child; help this champion process the event or the truth and support the integration of faith. Be available and mark the milestone. Just like Mary treasured "all these things" in her heart, you can treasure these as well. Treasure them and allow your child to place them in the proper perspective.

Ages 12 to 16

Your child is entering adolescence. Hold on to your hats! Just as there are more avenues of temptation for your child, there are more ways of escape for your child to learn and grow from. This is really where your child learns to walk by faith. They must have faith in God, faith in you, and faith in themselves.

This is also where your child learns about grace. Before a child sins, grace is just a concept. After your child sins, grace is a reality. As a parent, your ability to extend grace will enhance your child's ability to understand it from God's perspective. For if you can forgive and encourage your child to learn from his or her mistakes, it makes the truth of a compassionate, gracious God that much more real. It will also make the act of grace that much more amazing. Your child by this age knows that he or she sins and that you do. When you give grace, you do so from the platform of a fellow sinner. When God gives grace, He does so from the platform of righteousness. If you — a fellow sinner — reject your child and refuse to give grace, it makes it that much more impossible for your child to believe that a righteous God will extend grace.

Navigating grace and boundaries is not an easy task and I have one or two anxious thoughts myself about it, as I anticipate the aging of my boys. I'm not there yet, but I've had the privilege of watching friends, families, and colleagues negotiate this knife's edge of wisdom. I've also watched how grace and boundaries and their application have played out in the lives of those I've counseled. Through all of that, I've picked up a couple of things about adolescents along the way.

• *Adolescents still need boundaries.*

Yes, they are experimenting and testing, trying and experiencing, but underlying these needs to be a foundation of safety, of consistency, of love. If that foundation is shaky, they're much more likely to fall into temptation. Though they whine, complain, and push, keep the boundaries clear, concise, consistent, and reasonable. If they're movable, or there one minute and gone the next, they aren't boundaries, they're obstacles, and your teen will view them as such and work mightily to take advantage when they're not there and find a way around them when they are.

• *Adolescents need to be allowed to make mistakes.*

How will our children ever learn about grace if there's no need for it? Now, this is a truth really for us parents, not for kids. They already know they can and will make mistakes. We parents need to remember mistakes will happen. After all, this is a spiritual training exercise our children are engaged in. The only way to keep them from getting dirty, taking a knock or two, scraping a knee, or twisting an ankle is to pull them from the arena altogether. If you do, kiss the training goodbye, at least while they're under your roof.

Keep active, keep on the sidelines, keep aware of the game and how it's going, keep alert to the other players on the field, but let your kids play the game. Trust them to take a time out and run off the field to get instructions, ask questions, or receive a pat on the back when they need it. Call time out yourself, if needed, but recognize you've only got so many of them before you're going to be called yourself for delay-of-game.

• *Adolescents need to experience a team.*

You're the dad coaching from the sidelines. You're the mom cheering from the stands. You are not your adolescent's teammate. You're not your child's buddy or best friend; they have other people to fill those roles. You may and will, by God's grace, become your child's dear friend, as well as parent, later on in life, but do not expect it now.

Your child needs to be part of a team and who your child chooses to team with will tell you a great deal about how he or she is doing spiritually. It is appropriate for you to ask questions about who your child is "teaming" with. It is appropriate for you to make changes to your child's team, but if you pull your child from one team, you must help your child incorporate another — and it can't be just you and your family. That may seem safer, but it's not realistic and it doesn't help your child learn to operate in the arena of peers.

• *Adolescents need their space.*

Don't react to their growing independence by tying them tighter and tighter to you. This is dependence on you and it will hobble God's champion. Instead, this time of adolescence is meant to foster independence from you and a greater dependence on self and God. You cannot keep kids from wanting their space, but you can encourage them to make sure that space includes God.

• *Adolescents demand split-second timing.*

On the cusp of childhood and adulthood, this age vacillates back and forth. As a spiritual coach of this fluctuating champion, be aware that you'll need to learn how to read your child. Because of the immense physical and emotional changes happening during this stage, what your child needs from you at any given moment is a moving target. You must be prepared to be father or friend, mother or mentor, parent or peer. You must be prepared to spend at least an hour talking with your teen or accept barely a monosyllabic answer to the most complex question. You must be prepared to dive in and rescue your drowning child or wave calmly from shore as the waves roll in. You must be alert to, aware of, and available to your adolescent at any time, and on their schedule, not yours.

Insight and spiritual revelations — as well as just lessons about life in general — don't happen on a scheduled basis. For most of the parents I've spoken to, they describe adolescence as akin to sleeping on a bed of nails. I'm getting ready now to lose a little sleep.

• *Adolescents need the right armor.*

We've talked about that wonderful passage in Ephesians on the armor of God. We all understand how important it is for our teens to develop spiritual armor in order to be prepared to take on adulthood and the world. What we fail to understand as parents is that spiritual armor is not one-size-fits-all. All we have to do is take a look again at the story of when David met Goliath.

Do you remember how everyone, from Goliath to the other Israelites, thought it was absolutely ridiculous for a "boy" to come out to fight the giant of the Philistines? I'm making an assumption about the age of David but I'd say it was probably around the later part of this range. He was old enough to tend sheep and take food out to the battle lines, but not old enough to join in the battle himself. Do you remember what King Saul wanted to do when he heard that David was willing to fight Goliath? He didn't try to talk him out of it, but he did try to talk him into wearing someone else's armor.

Have you ever done that yourself with your adolescent? You know there's a battle coming up, you know you're willing for him or her to enter the arena, there's just one condition — they need to fight the battle your way. While this might seem loving to do, it presupposes a couple of things: 1) your child actually needs your kind of armor for the battle, and 2) your armor will fit. In the battle against Goliath, David had no need of Saul's armor. He already knew how he was going to defeat Goliath — through God's help and using the skills God had already given him. David was not trained as a warrior; he was trained as a shepherd. A shepherd's armor, not a king's, was sufficient for this battle. It wasn't Saul's mighty armor that was going to protect David and defeat Goliath. For this battle, David needed to travel light — just a slingshot and a few smooth stones.

Even if David had wanted Saul's armor to protect him, it was too big. It was too heavy. Saul's armor simply didn't fit David. Instead, David had to rely upon the armor of God's protection. There are battles our children must face for which our armor won't fit. It won't be appropriate for the battle. It's too big and too heavy. It was made specifically for us. Instead, our child must rely on the special, individual armor God has chosen for him or her. It may look like ours and it may not. We must resist the temptation to burden our children with our armor, and allow God to craft armor that's just right for our child and the situation.

It wasn't the armor that saved David, it was God. As parents, that's really all our children have to rely on. We can teach them and tell them what's right, we can model and manipulate circumstances to the best possible advantage, but ultimately it's not our righteousness or our children's righteousness that's going to save them. The only thing that will save them is being clothed in Christ. And the teen who is able to grasp that message, understand its meaning, and put this spiritual truth to the test in his or her own life is truly a champion for God, ready to conquer the world for Christ.

Ages 16 to 21

Why through age 21, when they graduate high school at 18? Because school is an artificial edge. I think young adults are still young until they're into their twenties. Just how far into their twenties really becomes individual to each person. Young men mature later than young women in general. I also put age 21 because it can be extremely difficult for young people after they graduate from high school. Whether they're off to college or not, they are no longer in the cocoon called high school. When they're no longer in that cocoon, they realize just how much of a cocoon it was.

At this stage, young people often obtain employment or work in volunteer positions, gaining experience for after high school. They're driving, earning their own money, and experiencing greater and greater independence from their parents — if not monetarily then certainly physically and emotionally. It is also a time of spiritual separation. This young champion you've just spent the last 16-plus years of your life molding may suddenly have questions or doubts about his or her faith. They may continue their journey of faith but seek out a different congregation or church denomination. If they attend school away from home, this will certainly be the case.

You are now definitely on the sidelines. While they're still in high school, you can do a lot more directing, but you're still on the sidelines. Actually, that's where you're supposed to be. You're like a special team coach on a football team. A special team coach gets to do a lot of work with individual players during practice. Once the game begins, the calls are being made by the head coach, whose strategies may or may not be understood or appreciated by the special team coach. The head coach may choose plays that highlight one special team over another, or he may choose to only use a special team for a limited amount of plays during any given game. It may seem like a special team is going to waste, languishing on the sidelines, when the head coach is waiting for just the right opportunity to use those players. That can be frustrating to those coaches and those players. The final call, however, remains with the head coach.

It can also be incredibly nerve-racking to be a special team coach, on the sidelines during the big game. You can't be out there, directing the players. Rather, they must use the knowledge you've given them and the skills they've gained to run the plays effectively. You want them to perform well, but you know they'll make mistakes. You just hope the opposing side doesn't take too much advantage of those mistakes. Regardless, you're there on the sidelines after each play, doing what you can to motivate and encourage, but knowing it's their game to play, not yours.

Here are some ways you can support these young people:

- *Consistent Faith*

I think of all the support you can give to young people in this stage of their lives, the most important is your consistent faith. This isn't the time to be drafting new plays on the sidelines. These young people need to be able to look to you and see the steadfast expression of your faith being lived out on a daily basis. So much of their lives is in a state of flux and you must be the constant. Your love, your example, your accountability, must be a rock for them to anchor to. This isn't to say you're a replacement for God, because you're not, but even Paul told the new Christians in Corinth to "follow my example, as I follow the example of Christ" (1 Cor. 11:1). Paul was not saying, "Follow me not Christ"; he was saying, "Follow me as I follow Christ." Your older teen needs to see you following Christ as consistently and as faithfully as you've done throughout his or her life.

- *A Willing Ear*

Notice, I didn't say a willing mouth. At this point in their lives, they've probably heard everything you've had to say — ten times over. If given the chance, they could compose your lecture for you, delivering your standard "lines" with just the right intonation and inflection. What they need is a willing ear. They need you to let them do the talking and just listen to them. Often, all they need is a sounding board, to test out what the truth they know sounds like, feels like. They know what's right, they just need to try it on for size first.

James 1:19 says, "My dear brothers, take note of this: Everyone should be quick to listen, slow to speak and slow to become angry." Did you catch that last part? If we're ever to have continuing influence over these champions for God who come to us for guidance, we must keep our anger in check. Our anger can be inflamed by fear. We're fearful of losing influence. We're fearful of our kids experiencing adult consequences. We're fearful of the battle laid out before them. We need to take the admonition of James to heart, especially when having those deep, meaningful conversations with our older children.

- *A Reaffirmation of Belief*

This is not a reaffirmation of a belief in God but rather a reaffirmation of your belief in your child. This is a reminder to make sure you bestow a blessing on your older child, especially at the point he or she is ready to live out from under your roof. Although they are excited about the prospect, they're also nervous about the outcome. Your faith affirms the best part of them. This is what you must continue to support. It's a way of projecting expectations, without being judgmental. If you tell your son, "I know you'll make good decisions while you're away at school," or tell your daughter, "I trust your decision to move in with Tracey because I know you understand how important it is to live a godly life," you've affirmed not only their decision but their core values. You've expressed your belief in their ability to do the right thing.

- *An Open Door*

While your older child may be ready to leave the nest, he or she needs to know you won't lock the door on their way out. There's that classic joke about a kid going off to school who comes home only to realize the parents have moved and left no forwarding address. No child wants to suffer the consequences of the Prodigal Son (though many will be tempted by the type of wild living spoken of this parable in Luke 15:11–31). However, every child wants to know that his or her parents will be like the father, who never stopped waiting or hoping for his son's return. It is not the wish of our young people to return home, once they've left, but they need to know they can. This is, after all, one of the most beautiful examples of how God loves us. His door always opens; all we need to do is knock.

In the last chapter of this book, called *Where to Go from Here*, there are two books that I think are tremendous resources for this stage of champion. Both are by Dr. James Dobson. The first is called *Life on the Edge* and the next is *Life on the Edge: The Next Generation's Guide to a Meaningful Future*. These are Dr. Dobson's thoughtful, godly presentations of the perils and promises of a life lived as a champion of God. If your children are older, I encourage you to get these books. If your children are younger, start now and read them yourself. This stage is pivotal, not only for your child, but for our culture and the Church.

This truly is the *next generation*. All we need to do is look at the history of the nations of Israel and Judah to realize how quickly — within a generation — the truth can be lost. We may not know all of the things God has in mind for our children, but one thing we do know — our children are meant to carry the torch of truth into the next generation.

Center Stage at Any Stage

No matter what the age of your child, you are called to support his or her molding into God's champion. This is a calling, a mission, a ministry. It's also an incredible joy and privilege. At any stage along the way, make sure God is center stage in the life of your child and your family.

Enjoy the time you have. Those who are parents give out all kinds of advice and have many different opinions and interpretations. There is one common element when you speak to parents — of any stage — and that is the time goes by far too quickly. We all get to do this once — until we, Lord willing, become grandparents — and even then it's a totally different experience (or so I'm told, by one Larry and one Judy Jantz).

Training Ground

Think about each of your children. What stage is he or she in? Which one is coming up? I want you to take a piece of paper and write down the following, replacing the blanks for each child's name:

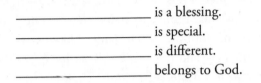

_____ is a blessing.
_____ is special.
_____ is different.
_____ belongs to God.

Now, under or beside each statement, write down ways you are communicating that message right now, today. Then, look over your list. It had better be pretty long. You should have written all over the paper and in the margins. If not, if it's pretty sparse, you've got some work to do.

Next, write down ways you can start today to communicate those messages in a more meaningful way. Think about each child, about what connects with that child, what is appealing to that child, and what is frustrating. Fine tune the message to your child's frequency. Be aware that your child may be coming up on a transitional age, perhaps entering school, puberty, or young adulthood.

Now, take just a moment and write down all the things you love about your child at this age. Cherish the moment; it will not come again.

Father, help me to love my child right now, today. Please don't let me spend too much time reminiscing about the past or spend too much time dreaming about the future. Today is all I really have with my child. Let it be enough. Let me show Your love, care, and compassion to my child today. If You will give me a tomorrow with my child, help me to use the time wisely, building my child up for the future You have in store.

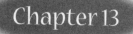

Chapter 13

Support for the Challenging Child

What do you think? If a man owns a hundred sheep, and one of them wanders away, will he not leave the ninety-nine on the hills and go look for the one that wandered off? (Matt. 18:12).

et's face it; it's easier for the challenging child to wander off. In our household, Benjamin is the challenging child. Headstrong, independent soul that he is, he's apt to become focused or distracted or just plain disobedient, and wander off. So, we have to watch him more carefully than Gregg at his age. This doesn't mean I love Benjamin any less. Rather, I accept Benjamin for who he is and make adjustments to my parenting to accommodate his personality. I don't say to God, "Why didn't you make Benjamin more like his brother?" Instead I pray, *Thank You, God, for giving me such different and unique children. As I love and parent them, they allow me to understand You in even greater ways.*

In a spiritual sense, we are all challenging children to God. Let's go back for a minute to the story of the Prodigal Son, found in Luke 15:11–31. This is called the Prodigal Son, but it's really the story of two sons, two brothers, both of whom had challenges. Let's look at the younger brother first, since in some ways he's the most famous. His problems were much more obvious. Scripture says he was headstrong — he actually went to his father and asked for his inheritance before his older brother. Then, he plans out his exit from the family and takes off for parts unknown. There, he squanders the money on "wild living." This son's shortcomings are obvious — he's impulsive, selfish, and headstrong.

What about the other son in the household? The parable portrays a dutiful son, who stays by his father and attends to the family. Sounds pretty good, right? Well, if you really look at the story, he's also willful, unforgiving, and jealous. Upon hearing that his lost brother is home, after being presumed, at least by his father, as dead, he isn't the least bit happy, joyful, or thankful. Instead, he's angry at his father. More, he's ungrateful, telling his father that the love and attention he's been given over the years is nothing more than "slavery." Instead of being grateful for all his father has provided for him, he's mad because he never took the initiative himself to kill a fattened animal and throw a party for his friends. Doesn't sound so "model" now, does he?

By the time the parable ends, the younger son is repentant, grateful, and a changed man. He recognizes all his father has done for him and, expecting nothing, comes home to confess his sins to his father. The older son, by contrast, is reminded by his father to show love and compassion to his brother. Neither brother is perfect.

Neither are we. Neither are our children. We are all challenging to God and each one of our children will prove challenging at times. For some, they will require extra measures of patience, wisdom and forbearance. These are the children I want to speak about in this chapter.

The Challenging Child

I cannot imagine that the prodigal son just turned around one day and became difficult. Instead, I get the sense that this kid was pretty wild from the get-go. Given his actions as this story opens, I can imagine he was always testing the boundaries growing up, trying to figure out how far he could go and how firm the boundaries were. What else can we learn from this parable?

- None of this caused his father to love him any less. Even with all the turmoil this kid caused, his father remained steadfast in his love.

- His father never wrote him off. It sounds like this kid was gone long enough that most everyone thought he was dead or at least would not return. Yet, the father continued to watch for him.

- His father waited for him to return. He did not follow him to bring him back. This is a gut-wrenching lesson and one I've seen many families agonize over. Their desire is to constantly drag home a difficult child turned adult. At some point, the only hope is for the child to return of his or her own volition, even if it means living for a while with pigs.

- The father did not neglect the son who stayed. The father did not use up the older son's inheritance in an attempt to gain back the younger son. This is an important, though incredibly difficult, point. When dealing with a challenging child in the family, an inordinate amount of family time, energy, and resources can be funneled into that child. At some point, this drain has a deleterious effect on the other family relationships. As much as the father loved the younger son, he did not allow that love to overshadow his love and care for the older son.

- The older son had his own issues with initiative. This is someone who stuck around the house. Yes, he didn't leave like his younger brother, but he so lacked initiative, he wouldn't even throw a party for his friends, unless his dad did it for him, and he blamed his dad for it.

- Even difficult children listen. Yes, the younger son had his epiphany in a pig sty, but at least he had it. He *remembered* what his father had said and demonstrated all those years growing up. It was in there, even if he didn't act like it. This is what gives all of us hope — for ourselves and for our children.

- Humility is the mark of repentance. When the younger son came back, he did not do so making demands. Instead, he humbly confessed his sin and asked for no special treatment, not even asking to be reinstated as a son. Challenging children can often be that way because they are able to charm the socks right off of you! It can be a challenge to know when their hearts have truly changed. This is one pivotal way — are they humble and repentant?

- Siblings will have their own, separate issues. Within the family structure, challenging children develop their own issues with their siblings. These issues are part of the family but reside outside of the relationship with the parents. Just because one relationship is mended does not mean the others will be as quickly or as easily.

The Emotionally Challenging Child

Challenging children are that way for a variety of reasons. Often, it's sheer personality. They are less settled, more active, more sensitive, than other children. They push against the boundaries and fight against the rules. Their spirits are more contentious. Quite frankly, they take more time and energy to corral.

Often what happens with this type of challenging child is that one of the parents ends up doing the heavy lifting. It may be the parent who is the most patient and can handle being tested without blowing a gasket. It may be the parent who is the disciplinarian, who views the child's behavior as a personal challenge to authority. It may be the parent who feels he or she must shield others from the effects of his or her child. Whatever the case, this is not a good situation. One parent should not be given the "duty" to deal with the challenging child exclusively. Rather, it should be a partnership, where parents work together, as a team, to help mold this child in godly ways. If you are a single parent with an emotionally challenging child, you will need to bring in reinforcements — extended family, special friends, or even behavioral specialists.

Watch for the type of challenge this child brings. If it's the exuberance of an active child, find lots of ways for him or her to blow off steam, to run and play, in order to achieve a state of calm. If the activity level just seems too frenetic, if the child has difficulty concentrating, staying on task, obeying rules, or being respectful, it's time to consult with professionals. In most cases, a structured, consistent routine, with expectations and consequences, can help these children choose to channel their energies in appropriate ways. In some cases, there may be a physiological component to their behavior such as ADD (attention deficit disorder) or ADHD (attention deficit hyperactivity disorder). While I believe there is an over-diagnosis today, especially among boys, of these conditions, for some they are very real and can be helped a great deal by thoughtful, professional medical management.

Sometimes children can be challenging for the opposite reason; instead of being too rambunctious, they are too passive, inactive, or apathetic. These children can tend to blend into the scenery and become overlooked. That's why it's important to have a read on all of your children and their emotional health. While it's natural for children to become disappointed or fearful, this should not be their natural state. Childhood is a time of discovery, exploration, and learning. These are positive, uplifting activities and children should respond accordingly. When they don't, it's time to find out why.

One of the key components of molding a champion for God is communicating a bright and positive future for your child. If he or she refuses to believe it or appears uninterested in the future, in activities, or playmates for an extended period of time, there may be an issue of depression. While this may sound very scary to parents, the wonderful news is there is help available through therapy and, in the small cases where it's appropriate, medication. Often, this type of behavior is linked to dietary choices that, when changed, can be extremely effective. Children with food sensitivities and allergies live in a body constantly at war with itself. Alleviating these conditions can help children to feel more at home in their bodies and more relaxed and optimistic.

One of the biggest areas of contention in the home can center around food. I see this all of the time at the Center. Challenging children are often those who refuse to eat, eat only certain foods, eat only at certain times, or generally exert their will at the table. At just the time the rest of the family is ready to relax and enjoy a meal, this challenging child is gearing up for a contest of wills or an expression of extreme frustration and anxiety. Again, this is not a natural state for children. You may be dealing with fear of food, sensory issues around texture or taste, disordered eating, or an eating disorder. If this does not resolve itself, or appears to be a pattern more than a phase, seek professional advice. Start first with your child's pediatrician, to determine if there is a physical reason for the behavior. Next, look to the food allergies and sensitivities mentioned earlier. Recognize that it may be necessary for you to consult with a counselor or therapist trained to work with children and food, weight, or sensory issues.

You may have noticed I've recommended several times to get professional help for a persistently challenging child. There's a reason for this: these children will drain you and your family. Their behavior can make it difficult for them to understand the types of spiritual lessons needed to navigate their own journey to faith and championship role for God. It's a classic case of getting off on the wrong foot. If you start a journey just a little bit off of where you're supposed to be and just keep going, you can end up miles away at the end. At first, it doesn't seem like that big of a deal, but over a lifetime, it can have tremendous consequences.

Get help yourself. Get help for your family. If your challenging child is really pushing the outer fabric of family cohesion, allow all the members of the family a safe place to process the strain this child produces. It does no good and much harm to demand that others in the family ignore the toll a truly emotionally challenging child can take.

The Physically Challenging Child

Sometimes the reason for the challenge is a physical one. Your child could have a physical or neurological condition, or a chronic disability or illness. The simple fact of caring for this child is demanding. In many of these situations, parents have come to recognize that God has called the family itself to be one of the first arenas for His champion to shine. Those children with a physical disability are often resilient, patient, and remarkably compassionate. This is a physically challenging child but a champion for God at an early age. Others in the family, when they rise to the occasion and treat this child with love and compassion, understand a deep, spiritual truth about God. These children may grow up to put this early lesson to great use in service to the Lord.

In the case of a neurologically challenging child, there may not be the depth of understanding on the part of the child. However, again, this situation can be used by God to temper the other champions under that roof. I have known several people who went into the caring professions, either nursing, therapy, or sign language, due to growing up with a disabled family member. It is not a given that this type of child will contribute only negatives to the family environment. On the contrary, this type of child can provide blessings to the family disguised at times as hard lessons.

It is important, when raising a challenging child, to be aware of the effects on the rest of the family and make adjustments as you're able. Again, seek professional help to navigate these adjustments. There are therapists trained in how to cope with physical, neurological, and developmental disabilities. Seek out a support group of others with similar situations, whose personal experiences — when added to your own — can provide creative and helpful solutions when possible, empathy and understanding when not possible.

The Home Front

With a challenging child, for whatever reason, your home becomes a battlefront, an arena for the Lord. This is true, of course, of all families, as we live out our humanity behind the porch screen door, but it's especially true of these families. How the family conducts itself — and each member individually — speaks a witness to the outside world of what Christians are made of. It highlights a life devoted to God. How you and your family respond is a parable in itself of the love of God and the power of faith. At times, this will be totally irrelevant to your pain and a lifeline on which to cling.

Don't give up hope. Claim the promise of Jeremiah 29:11 for yourself, your family, and your challenging child. God does know the plans He has for all of you, and it is a plan to prosper you and not to harm you, to give you a future and a hope. Your family may be a living descendant of the cloud of witnesses detailed in Hebrews 11, of which Scripture says, "These were all commended for their faith, yet none of them received what had been promised. God had planned something better for us so that only together with us would they be made perfect" (Heb. 11:39–40). In the desert of your challenge, it may seem that you are getting nothing of what was promised. Please know that God does have something better for us; His name is Jesus and He said, "My grace is sufficient for you, for my power is made perfect in weakness" (2 Cor. 12:9). Through your family, God is showing the strength of His power through your situation. I can only pray that God will make himself sufficient for you and that others will be called to aid you in your arena of faith.

Expect God to bless your family. Expect God to bless your challenging child. We do not know what tomorrow will bring. Just look at the difficult child born into the family of Mary and Joseph, their first-born. Always a little different, He seemed to march to the beat of a different drummer, even as a child. As an adult, He went about on such a crazy crusade even His brothers didn't believe Him. Though He was very learned and a gifted teacher, He kept saying radical things that stirred people up, and He wound up being arrested. Against all advice, He refused to speak up for himself at trial and ended up being killed by the ruling authority. This man was definitely a challenge for His whole family, and a Savior to the world. So, don't give up on that challenging child. You do not know what God is grooming him or her for. The ride will be bumpy, but you don't know the destination yet. Have faith. Teach faith. Model faith. You may be called to a Hebrews 11 kind of life.

Training Ground

If you have a challenging child, it can be difficult to maintain a sense of perspective. Take a moment and list each child you have. Each will be challenging in his or her own way. On one side, write down the areas of challenge for your child. These could be personality challenges, emotional challenges, physical challenges. Next, take a moment and reflect on how you've personally been blessed by helping your child deal with these challenges. If you're having trouble coming up with any, consider James 1:2–4 which says, "Consider it pure joy, my brothers, whenever you face trials of many kinds, because you know that the testing of your faith develops perseverance. Perseverance must finish its work so that you may be mature and complete, not lacking anything." If there is any blessing from your challenging child, it is the perseverance and faith you're gaining, helping you to attain a maturity in Christ.

For most parents, though, you're able to come up with many blessings you've gained, even from a challenging child. These children may be challenging, but they are not unlovable. Often there are aspects to their character and hearts that melt your own. Take some time to heal yourself with these.

Next, think about ways you can gain help in dealing with the challenges. Do you need to sit down as a family and re-strategize responsibilities or roles, in order to redistribute the load of a challenging child? Do you need to seek outside assistance from extended family or professional help? Is there a way you could reconfigure where you live or your daily responsibilities to take some pressure off?

Now, and most important, how can you reinforce the lessons from the last chapter? How can you communicate to your challenging child that he is a blessing in your life — that she is special

— that he is different — that she belongs to the Lord? Look for examples and stories in Scripture of parallels between your child and his or her situation and people of faith. Ask God to give you wisdom to use the common, ordinary events and challenges of the day to further your child's spiritual development.

Lord, help me not to resent this challenging child You've given me. Comfort me when I feel that way and guide me back to the truth. Give me strength and encouragement through Your Spirit and Your Word to face the challenge before me. Allow me to see my child through Your eyes — to glimpse the special future You are preparing for my child even now. Infuse me with hope. Help me to persevere. Increase my faith. Protect the love I have for this child and cause it to grow to fill up those times of despair and frustration. Thank You for loving and caring for this difficult child. Thank You for never leaving or forsaking me, no matter how challenging I am to You. May I emulate Your love for me to my own child. Heal me.

Chapter 14

Where to Go from Here

Finally . . . whatever is true, whatever is noble, whatever is right, whatever is pure, whatever is lovely, whatever is admirable — if anything is excellent or praiseworthy — think about such things (Phil. 4:8).

I commend you for reading this book, working through the exercises, praying the prayers, and committing yourself to the awesome ministry of raising up champions for God. Frankly, all of us need more champions on the fields of battle of this world. We need them at home, in the schoolhouse, at the workplace, in business, in politics, in ministry, and church. As Jesus reminded us in Luke 10:2, "The harvest is plentiful but the workers are few."

He then goes on to say that we are to "ask the Lord of the harvest, therefore, to send out workers into his harvest field."

Our children, God's champions, are those workers, and the harvest field is the redemption of souls. There is no greater ministry your child can be called to than this. God knew this and He planned for it. He planned, since before the foundation of the world, to call your child into service for Him, in this grand adventure of faith. Again, I commend you for understanding this truth and dedicating yourself to doing what's needed to realize its completion.

So much of Scripture talks about God's plans coming to completion, and the term used is often "made perfect." When your child realizes his or her destiny as a champion of God, your child is "made perfect." Isn't that our deepest desire, as parents? For our children to be made perfect in Christ? You've come a long way through reading this book toward making that a reality, but the end of this book is not the end of this journey. It's time to plan out your next steps.

One of the greatest blessings of writing this book has been the opportunity to take a look at other resources available. I encourage you to look over this list and find the next step you're going to take. Molding a champion for God is an ongoing adventure. It doesn't stop here. Look for books that are specific to your situation or child. (If you do not have children yourself, look for books that are specific to a child or family you know.)

There are so many things competing for our time and attention in society today. You've made a commitment to your child, God's champion, through this book — don't stop now. I promise you that nothing you devote your time to — television shows, hobbies, work, activities, the busy-ness of everyday life — will reward you as much as watching your child emerge as the champion he or she was meant to be.

For those of you who are bibliophiles, you'll enjoy just reading through the entire chapter, just to see what books are out there. For those of you who are a bit more selective, I've roughly grouped these resources according to the corresponding chapter in *Molding of a Champion.* I urge you not to limit your search; a toddler today is a teenager tomorrow, so keep it handy!

Ask God to alert you to specific books or themes He wants you to explore next. These are by no means all of the resources available, but those that caught my eye and my heart as I was preparing this book. Some of them are considered "classics," and for good reason. Others have been written quite recently. All have something to add to the conversation and, with guidance through the Spirit, can be of value to you in your sacred duty of helping to mold a champion for God and Christ.

Chapter 1: Preparing Yourself

Bringing Up Kids Without Tearing Them Down by Dr. Kevin Leman (Nashville, TN: Thomas Nelson, Inc., 1995). This is a wonderful parenting book. I just love the title — your champion needs to see him or herself as a champion. If you tear down your children, it will be difficult for them to see themselves as a champion. Perhaps one of the greatest strengths of this book is the ways it will help you take an honest look at your own parenting patterns and learn how to keep the good and jettison the bad.

I Love This Thing Called Parenting . . . Well, Most of the Time by Wendy Treat (Seattle, WA: Casey Treat Ministries). This book is worth reading just for the chapter entitled, "Fifteen Ways Parents Influence by Example." Wendy's got lots more in this book, written primarily to moms.

Moving Beyond Depression: A Whole-Person Approach to Healing by Gregory L. Jantz, Ph.D. (Colorado Springs, CO: Waterbrook Press, 2003). I put this book I wrote a couple of years ago in the section about preparing yourself. Depression in you can hinder your ability to parent your budding champion of God. This is an active, energetic pursuit, and depression drags down not only you but the rest of your family. If you recognize a pattern of lack of energy and motivation for an extended period of time, I encourage you to pick up this book and investigate the whole-person recovery that's possible.

Raising Great Kids by Dr. Henry Cloud and Dr. John Townsend (Grand Rapids, MI: Zondervan Publishing House, 1999). This is a book on character development from the team that brought us the *Boundaries* series. It's divided into well-defined chapters, defining essential character into six traits: connectedness, responsibility, reality, competence, morality, and worship. Though written several years ago, it's still one we recommend highly for parents at the Center.

The Power of a Praying Parent by Stormie Omartian (Eugene, OR: Harvest House Publishers, 1995). This book has become my constant companion, now that I have children. It is part of my devotional life, as I am reminded how important it is to be actively praying for my children. Stormie has a way of putting into words even the most difficult prayers. Let them inspire you in your own prayers, or use her thoughts to direct you as you pray for your child.

The Success Principles by Jack Canfied (New York, NY: HarperCollins Publishers, 2005). Written by the co-author of the *Chicken Soup for the Soul* series, this book is definitely not light reading or for kids! However, it definitely has value for adults! The joy of this book is the gain that you receive can be transferred to your child, through you. I suggest reading a chapter a week and taking time to discuss the principles with your child, in an age-appropriate way, of course. These are the kind of lessons that are perfect for sharing as you and your child walk through life together.

Chapter 2: Preparing Your Family

Becoming Strong Again by Dr. Gregory L. Jantz, Ph.D. (Grand Rapids, MI: Fleming H. Revell, 1998). It's not a quick, easy task to prepare your family to nurture the champions within. After reading this chapter, or even this book, you may doubt if you have the energy, the drive, the simple stamina for the job. I want to assure you that God is able to empower you in this area. It may be you need a little bit of what this book has to offer. It's subtitle is *How to Regain Emotional Health*. As the person who picked up and read this book, you're probably the caretaker of the family. This can be a rewarding, yet exhausting, role. Take some time to refresh yourself through this book!

Family Life by Leon Fontane of Springs Church (springschurch. org). This seven CD series is designed to strengthen your family life. It includes audio instructions on how to bring God into your marriage and home, as well as how to build your home through prayer. If you're not the sort to sit down and read, try ordering this CD set to listen to in your car or at home.

Healing the Scars of Emotional Abuse by Dr. Gregory L. Jantz, Ph.D. (Grand Rapids, MI: Fleming H. Revell, 1995, 2003). The latest version of this book is revised and updated from the one I wrote around ten years ago. The damage done by emotional abuse continues to resonate in our culture, so this book is still a needed resource for many. It's especially helpful for those whose own parenting has been adversely affected by the abusive patterns of their own parents. If you find yourself sounding and acting like your parents in negative, damaging ways, reading through this book can be a journey of personal discovery and healing, allowing you to unhinge yourself from your painful past and give your children a different, positive future.

Grace-based Parenting: Set Your Family Free by Dr. Tim Kimmel (Nashville, TN: Thomas Nelson, Inc., 2004). In order for your family to embrace the champions within, a basis of love and grace must be established — and this is a great resource toward that goal. I wouldn't say that anything in its pages is earth-shattering but it's just a helpful, common sense presentation of simple, biblical truths. Dr. Kimmel's style is conversational without being pedestrian. I liked his personal examples.

Family First: Your Step-by-Step Plan for Creating a Phenomenal Family by Dr. Phil McGraw (New York, NY: Free Press, 2004). Written by the popular Dr. Phil McGraw, I like this book for a couple of reasons: one, it was a *New York Times* best seller, so it shows that people in this country are interested in family; and two, for the section on purposeful parenting. It's not a Christian book, but it's a moral book, and worth a read.

The Blessing: Giving the Gift of Unconditional Love and Acceptance by John Trent, Ph.D. and Gary Smalley (Nashville, TN: Nelson Books, 1993). This is the revised and updated version of Trent and Smalley's classic book *The Blessing*, first published in 1986. It begins with "an important word to a new generation of parents," but even if you're one of the older generation, this book is worth reading again. The simple concept of passing on the blessing to our children resonates as strongly as it did 20 years ago. Haven't read it? It's time! Haven't read it in a while? It's time to read it again.

Chapter 3: Preparing Your Child

Boundaries with Kids by Dr. Henry Cloud and Dr. John Townsend (Grand Rapids, MI: Zondervan Publishing, 1998). Part of the *Boundaries* series, this book is a practical, important book for all parents. The subtitle of this one is *When to Say YES, When to Say NO, to Help Your Children Gain Control of Their Lives.* Divided into three parts, you'll learn why kids need boundaries, ten boundary principles kids need to know, and how to implement boundaries with kids. A healthy understanding of boundaries and how these work in the real world is invaluable to a budding champion of God. When I read this, I had notes and post-its everywhere! Helpful for any parent's library.

Chapter 4: Identifying Universal Gifts

Children Matter: Celebrating Their Place in the Church, Family, and Community by Scottie May, Beth Posterski, Catherine Stonehouse, and Linda Cannell (Grand Rapids, MI: Wm. B. Eerdmans Publishing Co., 2005). Many people contributed to the writing of this book (including Scottie May, who I was privileged to meet). If you enjoy an academic, comprehensive read, this book is for you. It's a detailed discussion of the spirituality of children and why the church should stop just babysitting children and start recognizing their amazing spiritual gifts.

Chapter 5: Identifying Personal Gifts

Addiction Approval: Overcoming Your Need to Please Everyone by Joyce Meyer (New York, NY: Time Warner Book Group, 2005). This may seem like a strange selection, but I really liked two chapters in this book which is essentially about accepting who you are: Chapter 2, "Knowing Who You Are" and Chapter 5, "Loving Yourself." We know from Paul's first letter to the Corinthian church that it's a human tendency to rate worth by gifts. I encourage you to read this book if you or your child has difficulty accepting the gifts that God has given him or her, especially if they're not exactly what you were expecting.

Chapter 6: Whole-Hearted

Emotional Intelligence by Daniel Goleman (New York, NY: Bantam Books, 1995). At over 300 pages, this book covers a lot of ground, but it's been one of the most influential in my personal life over the past several years. If more people grasped the concepts in this book, I'd have a lot less work to do. It's definitely not for kids, but your kids will benefit when you understand it yourself.

I Want to Teach My Child About Manners by Jennie Bishop (Cincinnati, OH: Standard Publishing, 2005). This is a fun little book that reminds all of us how important the simple things are in getting along with others. How we speak, behave, and treat others are discussed. It's an easy read with lots of colorful pages; the kind of book you could easily read and discuss with your younger child.

Raising an Emotionally Intelligent Child: The Heart of Parenting by John Gottman, Ph.D. with Joan Declaire (New York, NY: Simon and Schuster Paperbacks, 1997). This book, though sounding like Goleman's, is written from a different perspective. This book is written to encourage parents to become emotional coaches to their children. It outlines several parenting styles, both negative and positive. One of its more interesting features is the Emotional Awareness Self Test in chapter 3.

The Emotional Intelligence Quick Book by Travis Bradberry and Jean Greaves (New York, NY: Fireside, 2003, 2005). The authors of this book, based on the same concept as Goleman's book and Gottman's book, did research with over half a million people. Instead of being dry, this book is intentionally a distilled, quick presentation of the results, showing how important it is to master emotional intelligence.

Touchdown Alexander: My Story of Faith, Football, and Pursuing the Dream by Shaun Alexander (Eugene, OR: Harvest House, 2006). This autobiography by Seattle Seahawk Shaun Alexander is scheduled for publication in 2006. Personally, I can't wait to read it and discover even more that's amazing about my brother in Christ. I've put it in this section because Shaun has identified his personal gifts and is passionately, persuasively using them as champion for God on the football field and in every other field of his life. What a tremendous lesson for our own kids to read! Don't be fooled into thinking that because this book is about football that it's only applicable for boys. This is a football story, but it's also a faith story and about pursuing your dream for God. All children can be inspired and encouraged by Shaun's story.

Wow! Celebrations for the Successes of Life by Martha Bolton (West Monroe, LA: Howard Publishing, Co., Inc., 2006). This is a happy little party in a book — and the guest of honor is your child. Often, children have a hard time recognizing how special they are. This book is designed as an encouragement to your child. More appropriate to children pre-teen and younger, it's full of graphics and uplifting quotes. Each chapter celebrates some "Wow" to be experienced by your child. This is a perfect birthday or holiday gift.

Chapter 7: Spiritual Depth

Parents' Guide to the Spiritual Growth of Children: Helping Your Child Develop a Personal Faith by John Trent, Ph.D., Rich Osborne, and Kurt Bruner (Wheaton, IL: Tyndale House Publishers, 2000). This is a Focus on the Family book and is really a compilation of a variety of Christian authors. Its format is reminiscent of a text book and comes with "Keys to Success" and lots of "Hints and Helps." There is a great appendix of memory verses on a variety of life lessons. It's a comprehensive presentation of information; a part of Focus's Heritage Builders series.

Transforming Children into Spiritual Champions by George Barna (Ventura, CA: Regal Books, 2003). Subtitled *Why Children Should Be Your Church's #1 Priority*, it's written to church leadership and is

Barna's response to a realization that he'd missed the importance of children while researching the modern church. Not a long book, sometimes it's just good to read material from a trusted source that reinforces what you already know, from a very smart person.

Chapter 8: Intelligent Faith

Renewing the Mind: The Foundation of Your Success by Casey Treat (Tulsa, OK: Harrison House, 1999). I love this book, written by my pastor in Seattle, because it highlights the power of the renewed mind. Not only is it a good read for you, it's also appropriate for older teens and young adults.

Chapter 9: Strong in the Lord

God's Design for the Highly Healthy Child by Walt Larimore, M.D. with Stephen and Amanda Sorenson (Grand Rapids, MI: Zondervan, 2004). With a foreword by Dr. John Trent, you know this book has got to be good. Dr. Larimore combines solid biblical principles with medical knowledge. Ten essentials for nurturing highly healthy children make up the bulk of this book.

Healthy Food for Healthy Kids: A Practical and Tasty Guide to Your Child's Nutrition by Bridget Swinney (New York, NY: Simon and Schuster, 1999). Even though this book was written under the old Food Pyramid, it's still a good one, with an excellent discussion not only of food but foods that are good for kids. I appreciate its discussion of empty calories, additives, preservatives, and pesticides. There are quite a few easy-to-make recipes, created with young palates in mind. Because of where we are in our family, I found chapter 19, "Fun Snacks for Home and School" to be very helpful!

Healthy Habits, Happy Kids by Dr. Gregory L. Jantz, Ph.D. (Grand Rapids, MI: Fleming H. Revell, 2005). I recommend this book, not just because I wrote it, but because its whole-person emphasis is the perfect companion to this one. This book will help you strengthen your family and your family relationships. God's champion, your child, has been placed by Him within the context of your family, to grow and learn and mature. Help your family be fertile ground for this growth to occur.

Healthy Kids, Smart Kids by Yvonne Sanders-Butler, Ed.D (New York, NY: Penguin Group (USA), Inc., 2005). Recently, the local school district banned the sale of soda pop and high-calorie, high-fat foods in vending machines. This amazing revolution may owe its inception to the author who, as principal of a 1,000-student Georgia elementary school, went on a personal crusade to improve the health of her students and improve academic success. Her program, "Achieving Academic Excellence Through Nutrition" produced important results — lower absenteeism, higher attendance, better overall energy, and higher grades. Reading about her success can inspire you to achieve yours for your family.

Parents' Nutrition Bible by Dr. Earl Mindell, R.Ph., Ph.D. (Carson, CA: Hay House, Inc., 1992). This book may be older than many on this list but it's still a good one. If you're a parent who seems mystified by all of the various vitamins and supplements with unpronounceable names, this book is for you! It goes over vitamins and minerals in depth. There is also a section for parents whose child is allergic or food sensitive. A discussion of children's medicines and how to help kids heal faster from things like insect bites and acne is included. It's not a fancy book but it's very practical.

The Total Temple Makeover by Dr. Gregory L. Jantz, Ph.D. (West Monroe, LA: Howard Publishing Co., Inc., 2005). This chapter on physical health for your children may have brought to the surface issues you have yourself. In order for you to be on the same page with your children nutritionally, with the same goals and healthy eating, I encourage you to ask God to empower you to experience a total temple makeover. Your body is also a temple of God and this might be the right time for you to devote yourself to healthy living, for yourself and for your family.

Chapter 10: Support for Girls

The Wonder of Girls by Michael Gurian (New York NY: Atria Books, 2002). This book is not written from a Christian point of view, but I still heartily recommend it to every parent of a daughter. Gurian approaches girls from a nature-based platform, ascribing to nature that which God has designed. His research into female biology, neurology, and physiology is certainly controversial, but I found myself nodding my head in agreement more times than not. The subtitle is *Understanding the Hidden Nature of Our Daughters*. In that, this book delivers.

Chapter 11: Support for Boys

Bringing Up Boys: Practical Advice and Encouragement for Those Shaping the Next Generation of Men by Dr. James Dobson (Wheaton, IL: Tyndale House Publishers, Inc., 2001). Dobson starts this book out with a chapter entitled "The Wonderful World of Boys." Using personal experiences, biblical reasoning, and lots of letters from his radio programs, Dobson walks the reader through how to bring up boys in today's culture.

The Wonder of Boys by Michael Gurian (New York, NY: Penguin Putnam, Inc., 1996). The subtitle of this foundational book by Gurian is *What Parents, Mentors and Educators Can Do to Shape Boys into Exceptional Men*. Akin to his book on girls, this one speaks to the uniquely designed nature of boys. Gurian, while not ascribing that nature to a Creator, nonetheless gets many things right in this book. There is an entire chapter on teaching boys values, morality, and spirituality. This information, when interpreted through the lens of faith, can validate God's masculine design.

Too Close to the Flame: Recognizing and Avoiding Sexualized Relationships by Dr. Gregg Jantz (West Monroe, LA: Howard Publishing Co, Inc., 1999). Not specifically written to men only, this book is based on my years of counseling and the pitfalls of inappropriately sexualized relationships. Many churches have given this book to their pastoral staff and it has been a featured resource for Focus on the Family. In 2000, it received the *Angel Award* for adding a voice to the important cultural discussion of over-sexualization.

What Stories Does My Son Need? By Michael Gurian (New York, NY: Penguin Putnam, Inc., 2000). This book is an interesting collection featuring 100 movies and 100 books you can read or see with your son, along with a few thought-provoking questions to spur discussion. Gurian groups these resources into those appropriate for different age groups. It's a short, easy-to-read book that I found hard to put down. As I looked over his list, it was interesting to see what lessons he found in many of the classics.

Wild at Heart: Discovering the Secret of a Man's Soul (Nashville, TN: Thomas Nelson, Inc., 2001). This is a book for a male champion, as it celebrates the masculinity imbued by God. If you're a father, this book will revitalize your father-son bond. If you're a mother, I encourage you to read it and appreciate the special qualities your son embodies. For older boys, this would be excellent to either read alone or as part of a father-son reading project. Its deep concepts are just the stuff of adolescent dreams and yearnings.

Chapter 12: Support Across the Ages

Life on the Edge by James Dobson (Dallas, TX: Word Publishing, 1995). This book is subtitled *A Young Adult's Guide to a Meaningful Future*. Written for those ages 16 through 26, this is like a heart-to-heart talk for your child from one of the greatest Christian authors and thinkers of our age.

Life on the Edge: The Next Generation's Guide to a Meaningful Future by James Dobson (Dallas, TX: Word Publishing, 2000). This is a companion book to the above, written specifically to speak to the monumental decisions this age is confronted with: choosing a profession, choosing a pursuit, choosing a partner, and choosing a purpose. This book is an invaluable resource for God's champions, providing another strong voice in helping our older children make godly lifelong choices.

Putting a Face on Grace: Living a Life Worth Passing On by Richard Blackaby (Sisters, OR: Multnomah Publishers, Inc., 2006). This is just a gem of a little book, perfect for reading and discussing with your champion daughter or son. With its emphasis on grace, not only is it an opportunity to learn deep spiritual truths, but it should open up avenues of understanding between you and your teenager — at a very good time in both your lives.

The Dream Giver by Bruce Wilkinson with David and Heather Kopp (Sisters, OR: Multnomah Publishers, 2003). This is a fabulous book that encapsulates a very big idea in a little modern-day parable. This is the kind of book you can give to an older teen or young adult. It's engaging without being preachy and allows the reader to come to their own conclusions — perfect for this age.

The Five Love Languages of Teenagers by Gary Chapman (Chicago, IL: Northfield Publishing, 2000). This is just a great book for parents of teens to read and be reminded, yes — you really do love your children! Now my children are still quite young, but I work with teenagers every day and know how vitally important the lessons in this book are. If your child is nearing the teen years or is in the midst of full-blown adolescence, I highly recommend you pick this one up. Our teens need just as much love as our toddlers; we need to know how to speak to them in a way they will understand.

Chapter 13: Support for the Challenging Child

Four Weeks to a Better-Behaved Child by Cristine Chandler, Ph.D. with Laura McGrath (New York, NY: McGraw-Hill, 2004). I'm not sure about the four weeks part, but this book had many helpful suggestions. I especially liked the "4 Cs of discipline: clear, consistent, contingent, and consequences." The premise of this book is children respond best when they know exactly what's expected of them and are held accountable for their behavior. There is an especially helpful appendix that charts "how basic developmental abilities at each age impact discipline choices."

Caring for Your Grieving Child by Martha Wakenshaw, MA, LMHC (Oakland, CA: New Harbinger Publications, Inc., 2002). I am so pleased to recommend this book for parents whose child has suffered from grief or loss. It is written by my colleague at the Center, Martha Wakenshaw, whose foundational work with children and families touches and heals lives every day. Traumatic events can place significant barriers to your child understanding what it is to be God's champion. This book can help you navigate this difficult period and lovingly guide your child back on track.

Helping Gifted Children Soar: A Practical Guide for Parents and Teachers by Carol A. Strip, Ph.D. with Gretchen Hirsch (Scottsdale, AZ: Great Potential Press, Inc., 2000). This book helps answer the question, "Is my child gifted, or just smart?" Whether gifted or smart, these children can often represent a challenge to parents and the other adults in their lives. It's hard to stay two steps ahead with these kids! This practical book teaches parents about different learning styles and outlines some very "useful traits in working with gifted children" (pages 60–63). There is a helpful index at the back of the book for quick reference.

Kids, Parents and Power Struggles by Mary Sheedy Kurcinka (New York, NY: HarperCollins Publishers, 2000). This is a follow-up to the book listed below by the same author. It's full of practical suggestions for bonding with your intense, misbehaving child. You want to win the battle without defeating the heart of your child. At the end of each chapter, there is a section called "Coaching Tips" that I really appreciated.

Making Children Mind Without Losing Yours by Dr. Kevin Leman (Grand Rapids, MI: Baker Book House Company, 2000). Sometimes a challenging child is an independent little soul with a heaping helping of will. This is a great book (and a great title!) to help you corral that wild spirit, without crushing the life out of it. It's conversational and funny, with just the right blend of wit and wisdom.

No More Misbehavin': 38 Difficult Behaviors and How to Stop Them by Michelle Borba, Ed.D. (San Francisco, CA: Jossey-Bass, 2003). This book has an amazing list of 38 separate behavior challenges. Each chapter comes with a behavior tip and "Makeover Results" section, where you can document the progress you and your child are making.

Raising Your Spirited Child by Mary Sheedy Kurcinka (New York, NY: HarperCollins Publishers, 1992, 1998). The subtitle of this book is *A Guide for Parents Whose Child Is More Intense, Sensitive, Perceptive, Persistent, Energetic.* What Ms. Kurcinka calls *spirited,* others might call *difficult* or *strong-willed.* This excellent book will help you parents of spirited children to look at these traits as positives instead of negatives. I especially like the list of things "persistent spirited children need to hear" on page 114. If you're able to see the value of these character traits, you can communicate them to your child. For these children, the glass is definitely half-full not half-empty! This book helps parents appreciate their "diamonds in the rough."

The Out-of-Sync Child Has Fun: Activities for Kids with Sensory Integration Dysfunction by Carol Stock Kranowitz, MA (New York, NY: The Berkley Publishing Group, 2003). This is not a book for the timid, but if your child has dysfunction in sensory integration (DSI), it is for you. Here is how the author defines DSI: "The child who avoids ordinary sensations or seeks excessive stimulation, whose body is uncooperative, whose behavior is difficult, and who doesn't 'fit in' is our out-of-synch child (page 5)." A child with DSI can be a challenging, difficult child to relate to. Kranowtiz' book can help you learn to have fun with your child.

God, in His wisdom, has provided such wonderful resources for you, in this task of raising His champion. Take advantage of His bounty! Of course, do not neglect the foundation for these books, the Bible. Keep it close. Read it daily. Infuse your life, your thoughts, your attitudes, and your responses with the mind of God and Christ. May God bless you richly in this desire and allow you the joy and privilege of caring for His champions under your roof.

About the Authors

Dr. Gregg Jantz is the founder and executive director of the Center for Counseling and Health Resources, Inc., a Christian-based mental health and chemical dependency counseling agency with five locations in the Puget Sound area of Seattle, Washington. Married to his wife of 23 years, LaFon, they are the proud parents of two sons, Gregg and Benjamin. The author of over 16 books, his whole-person approach and dedication to the cause of hope touches hearts of readers and audiences around the country through his books and numerous appearances on radio and television. To learn more about Dr. Jantz and the healing work of the Center, please visit his website at www.aplaceofhope.com.

Ann McMurray is a freelance writer who also teams with Dr. Jantz as operations manager for the Center. Married for 28 years to her husband, Tad, they are the parents of grown children, Joel and Lindsay.